INTRODUCING
ISSUES WITH
OPPOSING
VIEWPOINTS®

Gay Marriage

Lauri S. Friedman, *Book Editor*

GREENHAVEN PRESS
A part of Gale, Cengage Learning

GALE
CENGAGE Learning·

Detroit • New York • San Francisco • New Haven, Conn • Waterville, Maine • London

Christine Nasso, *Publisher*
Elizabeth Des Chenes, *Managing Editor*

For more information, contact:
Greenhaven Press
27500 Drake Rd.
Farmington Hills, MI 48331-3535
Or you can visit our Internet site at gale.cengage.com

For product information and technology assistance, contact us at

Gale Customer Support, 1-800-877-4253
For permission to use material from this text or product, submit all requests online at
www.cengage.com/permissions

Further permissions questions can be e-mailed to permissionrequest@cengage.com

Articles in Greenhaven Press anthologies are often edited for length to meet page requirements. In addition, original titles of these works are changed to clearly present the main thesis and to explicitly indicate the author's opinion. Every effort is made to ensure that Greenhaven Press accurately reflects the original intent of the authors. Every effort has been made to trace the owners of copyrighted material.

Cover image copyright © Martin Ruetschi/Keystone/Corbis

LIBRARY OF CONGRESS CATALOGING-IN-PUBLICATION DATA

Gay marriage / Lauri S. Friedman, book editor.
   p. cm. -- (Introducing issues with opposing viewpoints)
Includes bibliographical references and index.
ISBN 978-0-7377-4734-8 (hbk.)
1. Same-sex marriage--United States--Juvenile literature. I. Friedman, Lauri S.
HQ1034.U5G38 2010
306.84'80973--dc22
                                                    2009052339

Printed in the United States of America
1 2 3 4 5 6 7 14 13 12 11 10

Contents

Foreword

Indulging in a wide spectrum of ideas, beliefs, and perspectives is a critical cornerstone of democracy. After all, it is often debates over differences of opinion, such as whether to legalize abortion, how to treat prisoners, or when to enact the death penalty, that shape our society and drive it forward. Such diversity of thought is frequently regarded as the hallmark of a healthy and civilized culture. As the Reverend Clifford Schutjer of the First Congregational Church in Mansfield, Ohio, declared in a 2001 sermon, "Surrounding oneself with only like-minded people, restricting what we listen to or read only to what we find agreeable is irresponsible. Refusing to entertain doubts once we make up our minds is a subtle but deadly form of arrogance." With this advice in mind, Introducing Issues with Opposing Viewpoints books aim to open readers' minds to the critically divergent views that comprise our world's most important debates.

Introducing Issues with Opposing Viewpoints simplifies for students the enormous and often overwhelming mass of material now available via print and electronic media. Collected in every volume is an array of opinions that captures the essence of a particular controversy or topic. Introducing Issues with Opposing Viewpoints books embody the spirit of nineteenth-century journalist Charles A. Dana's axiom: "Fight for your opinions, but do not believe that they contain the whole truth, or the only truth." Absorbing such contrasting opinions teaches students to analyze the strength of an argument and compare it to its opposition. From this process readers can inform and strengthen their own opinions, or be exposed to new information that will change their minds. Introducing Issues with Opposing Viewpoints is a mosaic of different voices. The authors are statesmen, pundits, academics, journalists, corporations, and ordinary people who have felt compelled to share their experiences and ideas in a public forum. Their words have been collected from newspapers, journals, books, speeches, interviews, and the Internet, the fastest growing body of opinionated material in the world.

Introducing Issues with Opposing Viewpoints shares many of the well-known features of its critically acclaimed parent series, Opposing Viewpoints. The articles are presented in a pro/con format, allowing readers to absorb divergent perspectives side by side. Active reading questions preface each viewpoint, requiring the student to approach the material thoughtfully and carefully. Useful charts, graphs, and cartoons supplement each article. A thorough introduction provides readers with crucial background on an issue. An annotated bibliography points the reader toward articles, books, and Web sites that contain additional information on the topic. An appendix of organizations to contact contains a wide variety of charities, nonprofit organizations, political groups, and private enterprises that each hold a position on the issue at hand. Finally, a comprehensive index allows readers to locate content quickly and efficiently.

Introducing Issues with Opposing Viewpoints is also significantly different from Opposing Viewpoints. As the series title implies, its presentation will help introduce students to the concept of opposing viewpoints and learn to use this material to aid in critical writing and debate. The series' four-color, accessible format makes the books attractive and inviting to readers of all levels. In addition, each viewpoint has been carefully edited to maximize a reader's understanding of the content. Short but thorough viewpoints capture the essence of an argument. A substantial, thought-provoking essay question placed at the end of each viewpoint asks the student to further investigate the issues raised in the viewpoint, compare and contrast two authors' arguments, or consider how one might go about forming an opinion on the topic at hand. Each viewpoint contains sidebars that include at-a-glance information and handy statistics. A Facts About section located in the back of the book further supplies students with relevant facts and figures.

Following in the tradition of the Opposing Viewpoints series, Greenhaven Press continues to provide readers with invaluable exposure to the controversial issues that shape our world. As John Stuart Mill once wrote: "The only way in which a human being can make some approach to knowing the whole of a subject is by hearing what can be said about it by persons of every variety of opinion and studying all modes in which it can be looked at by every character of mind. No wise man ever acquired his wisdom in any mode but this." It is to this principle that Introducing Issues with Opposing Viewpoints books are dedicated.

Introduction

With every passing year, the issue of gay marriage grows in controversy. In almost every election cycle, state ballot initiatives ban or bless same-sex unions, and state courts increasingly make rulings on the matter. Much of the debate over gay marriage focuses on how it would affect society if it were to be legalized—how it would affect children, the institution of marriage, and society as a whole. But as gay marriage becomes legal in more places, questions about how it would affect society become a little easier to answer. Massachusetts was the first state to legalize gay marriage in 2003, and as such is a good place to look for answers to these questions.

Although gay marriages have represented only about 7 percent of all state marriages since 2004, their legalization has impacted Massachusetts in several positive ways. One of these impacts has been financial: Massachusetts has experienced an economic boom as a result of same-sex weddings. Considering that the average cost of a wedding is between $20,000 and $30,000, gay couples have contributed millions to the industry and their state's economy, which has been especially helpful in the economic recession that began in 2007. One study by the Williams Institute at the University of California at Los Angeles School of Law found that between May 2004 and September 2008, almost half of married same-sex couples in Massachusetts spent $5,000 or more on their weddings, while about 10 percent spent more than $20,000. These weddings boosted the economies of the communities in which they were held when parties were booked at restaurants and out-of-town guests checked into hotels and rented cars. As a result, study authors estimated that same-sex marriages have contributed more than $111 million to the state economy since 2004.

Another positive effect of gay marriage in Massachusetts has been a lower state divorce rate. Five years after legalizing gay marriage, Massachusetts had the lowest divorce rate in the United States, according to data from the National Center for Vital Statistics. In fact, in 2008 its divorce rates were on par with what the nation's had been in 1940. This surprising statistic seemed to quell some opponents' fears that gay marriage would cause the disintegration of the traditional institution of marriage.

Finally, the lives of thousands of gay citizens have improved as a result of the Massachusetts law. For example, Kenneth Harvey, who married his partner Bruce Myers soon after gay marriage was legalized, says that being married has given him and his husband access to important state rights. When Harvey suffered a stroke in 2008, Myers was able to go to the hospital with him and enjoy the legal benefits conferred to spouses in medical emergencies. "Just being able to introduce (Myers) as my husband in the emergency ward was enormously comfortable," says Harvey. "Everyone knew who he was and he was immediately involved with the doctors' decisions."[1] Harvey says that legalized gay marriage has brought numerous such benefits to people like himself without affecting anyone else or harming greater society. Maureen Brodoff and Ellen Wade, who also married under the Massachusetts law, agree: "The sky didn't fall. The newness of it has eased," they said upon the five-year anniversary of gay marriage in their state. "[Ours] is just another marriage."[2] In fact, gay marriage has become so normalized in some Massachusetts communities that townships have stopped distinguishing gay marriages from straight ones and no longer keep records on the difference.

But opponents of same-sex marriage believe it is too soon to call Massachusetts's experiment with gay marriage a success. According to Maggie Gallagher, president of the Institute of Marriage and Public Policy, gay marriage will, over time, lead to a breakdown of civilized American society and threaten the welfare of children raised in same-sex households. Gallagher points to the gradual acceptance of gay marriage in Massachusetts as proof this is already happening. According to a poll commissioned by her organization, in 2004, 84 percent of Massachusetts voters said they believed it is better for children to be raised by their married mother and father. When the same question was put to them in 2009, just 76 percent of Massachusetts voters agreed. To Gallagher and other opponents of gay marriage, this represents a dangerous acceptance of a trend that they believe will ultimately harm the country. "Support for the idea that children need a mom and dad has dropped, and a substantial minority of people believe it is risky to oppose gay marriage openly,"[3] says Gallagher, and this deeply concerns her.

Others believe that gay couples have no use for marriage, and, once they get over the novelty of being allowed to marry, they will tire of the institution—but not before they have weakened it. A couple named Julie and Hillary Goodridge are proof of this for gay marriage opponents. Interestingly, the Goodridges led the fight for Massachusetts to legalize same-sex marriage in 2003—in fact, they were the plaintiffs in the landmark case *Goodridge v. Dept. of Public Health* that ultimately led to the legalization of same-sex marriage in that state. As such, the Goodridges were among the first couples to take advantage of the new law. Yet as Massachusetts was celebrating five years of same-sex marriage, the Goodridges were not—they separated in 2006 and divorced in January 2009.

Many opponents of same-sex marriage point to the Goodridges as an example of why gays should not be allowed to marry in the first place. Writer David Benkof, who himself is gay, says that gay unions should not be legalized because such relationships are not typically monogamous. "I argue against same-sex marriage in part because I think the gay and lesbian community barely understands marriage, particularly the part about fidelity,"[4] he says. Others argue that gay relationships tend to fall apart faster than straight ones—for example, the Family Research Council claims that while straight marriages last an average of twenty years, gay relationships last an average of a year and a half. For these and other reasons, opponents of gay marriage say it makes no sense to extend an institution to people who are going to disregard its very core tenets. They believe it is just a matter of time before Massachusetts and the other states in which gay marriage is legalized reap the negative consequences of this decision.

Whether same-sex marriage is good or bad for communities is at the heart of the many issues debated in *Introducing Issues with Opposing Viewpoints: Gay Marriage*. The wealth of information and perspectives provided in the articles that follow will help students come to their own conclusions about same-sex marriage and whether it should be legal in the United States.

Notes

1. Quoted in Jeff Gilbride, "Five Years of Gay Marriage—a Quiet Milestone," *Waltham (MA) Daily News Tribune*, May 17, 2009.

2. Quoted in David Filipov, "5 Years later, Views Shift Subtly on Gay Marriage," *Boston Globe*, November 17, 2008. www.boston .com/news/local/massachusetts/articles/2008/11/17/5_years_ later_views_shift_subtly_on_gay_marriage.

3. Maggie Gallagher, "Massachusetts Gay Marriage: Five Years Later," RealClearPolitics.com, May 20, 2009. www.realclearpolitics.com/ articles/2009/05/20/massachusetts_gay_marriage_five_years_ later_96579.html.

4. David Benkof, "Monogamous Same-Sex Adultery," *San Francisco Chronicle*, June 26, 2008.

Chapter 1

Should Gay Marriage Be Legal?

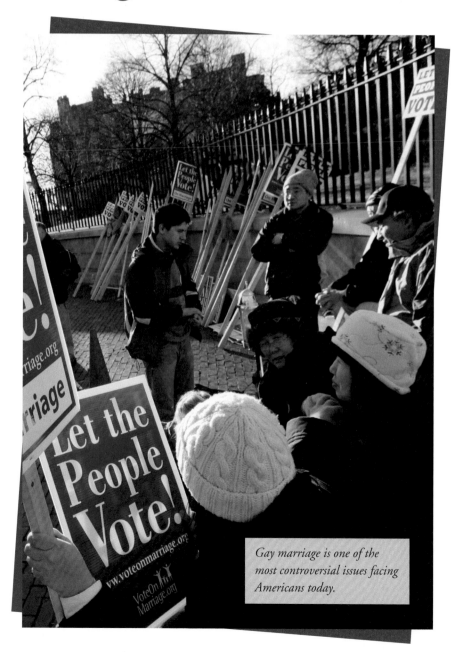

Gay marriage is one of the most controversial issues facing Americans today.

Viewpoint

1

Gay Marriage Should Be Legal

Lester Olson

Gay relationships are every bit as legitimate as heterosexual relationships, argues Lester Olson in the following viewpoint. For this reason, he thinks they should be legalized. To make his point, Olson tells the story of his own relationship with his partner, Keith. He says the qualities that make up their union—commitment, respect, love, shared values, communal money and property—are the same as those that make up heterosexual relationships. Yet because their union is not legalized, he and Keith have been discriminated against, denied benefits, money, and other rights. Olson says that gay marriage should be legalized because it helps families and individuals to flourish. In his opinion, this can only help society, and thus the government should be interested in legalizing these unions.

Olson is a professor at the University of Wisconsin, Madison.

> *"The government's recognition of same-sex civil marriage would move us toward a society that is more humane, inclusive, and compassionate."*

Vital Speeches of the Day, January 2009, for "Fool's Gold in California" by Lester Olson. Reproduced by permission of the author.

AS YOU READ, CONSIDER THE FOLLOWING QUESTIONS:
1. What percent of American children are raised in gay and lesbian households, according to Olson?
2. What is the main reason that Olson says the government has a compelling interest in supporting same-sex marriage?
3. How much does Olson estimate he and his partner, Keith, would have been denied in benefits compensation over the course of his thirty-year career?

Keith and I initiated our twelve-year partnership during Independence Day weekend in 1980. Yes, there were fireworks—a lot of fireworks, if you know what I mean. And each anniversary, the other sort of fireworks had a poetic, personal resonance for us, as did the immense crowds that showed up dependably to help celebrate.

A Relationship Like Any Other

Paradoxically, our commitment signified our freedom, independence, and liberty, as well as our pursuit of happiness. Most components of my partnership were not remarkably different from civil marriages, except, of course, that we could not legally marry each other. Sexual values, money management, sharing our resources, maintaining our health and well being, becoming helpmates, deciding whether to raise children together—we had to examine and discuss every component of our partnership. We decided with ambivalence against raising children. In contrast, a close friend, who formed his same-sex union about the same time, raised two sons. At one time, the American Bar Association estimated that about 8 percent of children in the U.S. are raised in gay or lesbian households.

Discrimination Still Exists in the United States

Same sex couples always have and always will form families—not only over the decades but across the centuries, not only in the U.S., but around the globe. In this country, we have done so with dignity and courage and grace under hostile conditions. The only crucial difference that bears scrutiny is the hostility of some, who imagine that their disdain for us has something to do with virtue. If you doubt that we deal with discomfort, contempt, and supremacy, often parading about as piety, consider the 52 percent of Californians who voted to assault our marriages, who battered our hopes, and shattered any illusions of equal inclusion in society—all under the pretense of "virtue."[1]

Now in a country that professes to deplore discrimination, this crucial difference is a powerful, additional reason for government support for same-sex marriages. It's called equal protection under the laws. It's called security of person.

There is no public reason for why government should recognize publicly heterosexual civil marriages that does not apply likewise to same-sex marriages. Indeed, government has a compelling interest for supporting both sorts of marriage for the same, simple reason: when families flourish—all families—then communities flourish, and when communities flourish, then states and nations flourish.

Accepting Gay Relationships

In my youth, recognition of my relationship by my family mattered to me far more than by Uncle Sam. So my . . . story concerns my parents, because, however personal, it underscores public values at stake in the marriage controversy. In 1984, after I secured my job at the University of Pittsburgh, my father asked me three direct questions in my mother's presence:

When I moved to Pittsburgh, he inquired, "would Keith be moving to live there too?" "Yes," I replied, "he would."

Then he asked me, would I be "living together with Keith there the way that we had been in Madison?" We had been living in an efficiency apartment. Secretly, I hoped for a bit more space. But that wasn't what he was asking me. "Yes," I responded, "we would."

Then my father inquired, did I "think about Keith the way that another person might a spouse?" This question made me nervous. Some years earlier, I had dated a man whose family disowned and disinherited him, when they learned that he was gay. This was not likely from my parents. But we were on unfamiliar ground. I had no idea where this was headed next.

---

1. The author is referring to a 2008 California ballot initiative that made gay marriage illegal.

Americans Are Coming Around to Gay Marriage

2009 marked the first time that more Americans believed it should be legal for homosexual couples to marry than did not.

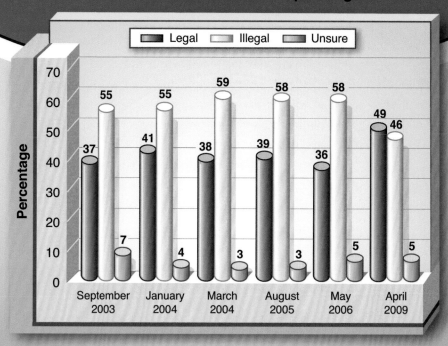

"Do you think it should be legal or illegal for gay and lesbian/homosexual couples to get married?"

Taken from: ABC News/*Washington Post* poll, April 21–24, 2009.

"Yes," I replied, "I do."

My father then turned to my mother and, demonstrably pleased, said, "It looks like we have another son." He immediately welcomed Keith into our family as "another son." My father only completed the eighth grade, because his family's material circumstances meant that he needed to work on the family farm. Now in his eighties, he still participates in his weekly men's bible study group. I hope you will agree that he has set a high standard for anyone, anywhere who wants to talk about the so-called "family" values.

Gay Marriage Reflects Important Public Virtues

Inclusion and acceptance, respect, honesty and openness, goodwill, generosity of spirit and resources, and, above all, love—these public values inhabit our side of this controversy. What our mistaken friends and hate filled adversaries on the other side of the question proffer is counterfeit virtue, fool's gold. Sadly, here in the Golden State too many voters apparently don't recognize the differences.

While my parents' recognition of my partnership was only one of many loving stories that I could share concerning my family, the last story is politically difficult to share with you. It concerns the ramifications of my employer's non-recognition of my partnership. It will be easy for you to misunderstand my last story. So I request careful listening.

Gay Partners Deserve Recognition

Shortly after Keith and I had settled into our Pittsburgh home, we decided to use the University recreational facilities. We went swimming. My married counterpart could bring a spouse plus all of the chil-

Gay couples believe that they are entitled to the same rights in marriage as those granted to heterosexual couples.

dren for free. But, for me to bring Keith, or anyone at all, I had to pay one dollar—not a large sum. But it was symptomatic of an extensive system of economic discrimination through my employer's benefits package, including life and health insurance, free tuition, recreation and library privileges for spouse and kids. Through the benefits package alone, I estimated that the difference in compensation over a thirty-year career exceeded a quarter of a million dollars. This was in the 1980s. And this figure did not include differences in actual salaries between single and married employees, which was significant, too.

Now it would be easy to misunderstand my point, because I do not begrudge others support for their committed relationships. We're all interdependent. We depend on each other all the time, albeit in different ways and to different degrees. And yet, there should be equal compensation for comparable labor without regard for marital status.

Toward a More Humane Society

Therefore, while the government's recognition of same-sex civil marriage would move us toward a society that is more humane, inclusive, and compassionate, it is not sufficient to enact our commitment to equality. Recognition of same-sex civil marriage will not be enough to assure equality between those who marry. Nor does it assure equality between married and single persons. We need to have difficult conversations concerning how to actualize equality.

In closing, I have suggested that the only crucial difference that bears scrutiny between publicly heterosexual and same-sex marriage is the hostility that same-sex couples encounter as self respecting U.S. citizens. I have suggested that this difference is yet another reason for government recognition for same-sex marriage. Same-sex marriage enacts a powerful form of visibility politics in life-enhancing ways, because honesty, openness, and communication can reduce prejudice.

Conservatives and liberals, reactionaries and radicals do have some things in common. One of them is that, across the political spectrum, people have decided to get married. We develop committed partnerships for some of the same reasons that we form communities, states, and nations. We are interdependent. We need each other. This is the most basic reason that government has any interest at all in civil marriage—to strengthen existing relationships between consenting, adult people. For that reason, I ask each of you to reflect on how you will use your privilege in the weeks ahead as the controversy over same-sex marriage continues. Let's commit, above all, to continuing the conversation. In a spirit of abiding hope, I will conclude with two lines from a poem by Audre Lorde:

> "We have chosen each other
> and the edge of each others' battles."

EVALUATING THE AUTHOR'S ARGUMENTS:

To make his point that gay marriage should be legal, Lester Olson tells a personal story from his own life. Identify the elements of this story and explain whether or not they helped convince you of his argument.

Gay Marriage Should Not Be Legal

Daniel R. Heimbach

"Under homosexual terms, marriage will be no stronger than feelings of private satisfaction."

In the following viewpoint Daniel R. Heimbach says there are many reasons to outlaw same-sex marriage. Although gay couples claim to love each other as much as straight couples do, Heimbach says the institution of marriage is about more than just love—it is about making and raising children, something that gay couples cannot do naturally and should not do at all since, in Heimbach's opinion, children raised by gay couples are prone to sexual confusion, depression, criminality, and drug abuse. Heimbach also rejects the notion that marriage is a universal right. Just as brothers cannot marry sisters and teachers cannot marry students, so too should gay couples be prevented from marrying simply because they want to. Heimbach concludes that marriage is not just about institutionalizing any kind of relationship, but only male-female ones that exist to strengthen society by sharing property and children.

Heimbach is a professor of Christian ethics at Southeastern Baptist Theological Seminary. He is also the author of the book *True Sexual Morality: Recovering Biblical Standards for a Culture in Crisis.*

Daniel R. Heimbach, "Why Not Same-Sex 'Marriage'? Responses to 10 Arguments for Same-Sex 'Marriage,'" *Findings,* January 1, 2009. Reproduced by permission of North Carolina Family Policy Council.

AS YOU READ, CONSIDER THE FOLLOWING QUESTIONS:
1. How would same-sex marriage hurt the already weakened institution of marriage, according to Heimbach?
2. Heimbach says that children raised by gay parents are far more
   likely to die of what?
3. What does Heimbach say the effect of same-sex marriage has
   been on Scandinavia?

T his article presents . . . the most common arguments for
same-sex "marriage" and responds to them logically, demonstrating why these arguments do not present a sound defense
of same sex "marriage.". . .

Marriage Is More than Love

*The Argument: Same-sex marriage should be allowed because marriage is
about love, and homosexuals love each other as much as heterosexuals. . . .*

The Response: This argument confuses a valued (but not a necessary)
motive for mate selection with what qualifies marriage to be recognized as a social institution. Love should characterize how married
partners treat each other, but love is not what structures marriage and
is not what warrants public interest in affirming marriage. The public
interest in marriage relates to how it moves toward bridging the male-
female divide, toward favoring procreation, and toward parents set-
ting aside individual satisfaction to cooperate in raising children. . . .

Gay Marriage Threatens an Already Weak Institution

*The Argument: Same-sex marriage should be allowed to save marriage
from the mess created by heterosexuals. Heterosexuals have done so poorly
at marriage, who are they to speak now? . . .*

The Response: It is true that nearly half of all new heterosexual marriages are now ending in divorce. But that also means that about
half do not, and that the rate of success is much higher if one counts
older as well as younger marriages. While this situation is bad, it does
not mean heterosexuals have no idea how marriages succeed. It only

shows that the younger generation is accepting destructive values and ideas that earlier generations did not.

It is a sad irony that proponents of this argument are adding fuel to the fire they would fix. They would have us accept *more* of the very idea causing the marriage crisis in the first place. That is, they would change the main reason for socially approved marriage from limiting personal desires in favor of procreation, to the socially destructive idea of valuing marriage by how it gratifies individual feelings and desires. The influence of the later idea is why marriage is in such trouble today, and same-sex marriage will make it worse, not better. Under homosexual terms, marriage will be no stronger than feelings of private satisfaction, and will cease to be an authoritative, pro-child institution encouraged to endure no matter how feelings fluctuate. When this happens, society will suffer because the families that form its basis lose their stability—an effect that will have repercussions for future generations. . . .

Hurting Children

The Argument: Same-sex marriage should be allowed because children need married parents, not necessarily fathers and mothers. It is better

The author asserts that a child raised by gay parents is prone to sexual confusion, depression, criminality, and drug abuse.

for children to be raised by parents who are married than are unmarried, and it makes no difference whether parents are heterosexual or homosexual. . . .

The Response: This argument proposes to keep the connection linking marriage to parenting but asserts the underlying idea that it is more important for adults raising children to be married than for children to have both a father and mother. Children will be adversely affected if the social structure of marriage is altered to make having both a father and mother something arbitrary, abnormal or even unnecessary for raising well adjusted children.

In reality, children raised by homosexuals do not do as well, but rather do worse, than children raised by heterosexual father-mother pairs. . . . On evaluating 49 empirical studies on same-sex parenting, Drs. Robert Lerner and Althea Nagai found no basis for supposing children raised by homosexuals do as well as others. Compared to others, children raised by homosexuals are at much greater risk of gender dissatisfaction, gender confusion, suicide, long-term depression, mood disorders, bipolar disorders, sexual promiscuity, out-of-wedlock pregnancy, and sexually transmitted diseases. Research shows they are also more likely than others (especially others raised by both a father and mother), to become criminals, to abuse drugs, to have poor grades, to be expelled, and to struggle with finding and keeping jobs. Sadly, they are also far more likely to die of maltreatment, or to be sexually abused by a member of their families, than children in households with two biological parents. . . .

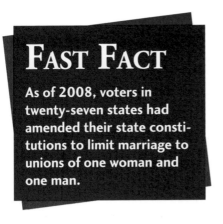

FAST FACT

As of 2008, voters in twenty-seven states had amended their state constitutions to limit marriage to unions of one woman and one man.

Marriage Is Not a Human Right

The Argument: Same-sex marriage should be allowed because marriage is a basic human right. Allowing homosexuals to marry like everyone else does not create a "special right" for homosexuals. Rather it only removes a barrier excluding gays from a basic right already available to everyone else.

The Response: Practical benefits given by law favoring marriage and family relationships have never been for affirming just any committed relationship at all. Many seriously committed relationships exist between friends, neighbors, classmates, or teammates that are not treated in the same category when it comes to benefits favoring marriage and family, and many sexual relationships also exist that do not qualify in the same category as marriage either. Prostitutes have no preferential right to inherit the property of customers, nor are they entitled for customers to list them as dependents on a tax form.

Marriage is not just any sort of committed relationship at all, and does not involve just any sort of sexual attraction at all. There is no such thing as a universal right to marry just any partner one happens to choose, or even to marry based on satisfying any attraction one happens to have. The right to marry is intrinsically linked to society's interest in procreation, and even though some couples never have children, their right to marry depends on the structure of an institution that aims at limiting procreational sex to couples committed to staying together long enough to raise children, and not merely at affirming whatever attractions anyone has regardless of that structure. . . .

Same-Sex Marriage Hurts Society

The Argument: Marriage is uniquely good for the stability and security of family life, and encouraging couples to marry recognizes and supports the value of forming families. Denying marriage to same-sex couples does not keep homosexuals from starting families, but it does hinder recognizing and supporting the value of their families. . . .

The Response: Successful, well-adjusted children are most likely to come from families consisting of a father and mother, and marriage is the best way of getting fathers and mothers to cooperate in raising children. Since children are the future leaders of society, society is best served if children have as many advantages as possible. Studies show that children raised by same-sex parents fare worse than children raised by a father and mother. Same-sex marriage diminishes the value of children to the family structure by stressing that while

Important Dates in the Fight over Same-Sex Marriage

1996

President Bill Clinton signs into law the federal Defense of Marriage Act (DOMA), which upholds states' rights to ban same-sex marriages and to refuse to recognize such marriages performed elsewhere.

1998

Alaska voters approve a constitutional amendment banning same-sex marriage.

2000

Vermont becomes the first state to legally recognize same-sex couples via civil union.

Nebraska voters approve a constitutional ban on same-sex marriage.

2002

Nevada voters give final approval to a constitutional ban on same-sex marriage.

2003

Massachusetts becomes the first state to legalize same-sex marriage. Weddings begin in May of the following year.

2004

Voters in thirteen states–Missouri, Louisiana, Arkansas, Georgia, Kentucky, Michigan, Mississippi, Montana, North Dakota, Ohio, Oklahoma, Oregon, and Utah–approve constitutional amendments banning same-sex marriage.

2005

Kansas and Texas voters approve constitutional amendments banning same-sex marriage.

Connecticut approves civil unions for same-sex couples

2006

Voters in eight states–Alabama, Idaho, Colorado, South Dakota, South Carolina, Tennessee, Virginia, and Wisconsin–approve constitutional amendments banning same-sex marriage.

New Jersey allows same-sex couples to enter into civil unions, granting them the same state benefits conferred on married couples.

2007

Oregon legalize domestic partnerships.

2008

In May the California Supreme Court rules that the state constitution guarantees same-sex couples the right to marry. Marriages begin but are quickly overturned in November, when voters approve Proposition 8, which decrees marriage as being between a man and a woman only.

Connecticut becomes the second state to legalize same-sex marriages.

2009

In the wake of the passage of Proposition 8, the California Supreme Court decides to uphold the legality of marriages conducted earlier in the year but prohibits any new same-sex marriages from occurring.

Iowa, Vermont, Maine, and New Hampshire legalize same-sex marriage. Maine voters repeal their state's gay marriage law November 4, 2009.

New York and the District of Columbia will not perform same-sex marriages but will recognize those from other states.

Washington passes the "everything-but-marriage" law, which grants domestic partners most of the same rights that spouses get.

marriage must satisfy adult feelings, its structure need not align with what children need.

Same-sex marriage is bad for family integrity, and especially for children, because removing the procreative form from marriage erases incentives encouraging parents (or potential parents) to accept restrictions best for raising children. Treating marriage as if nothing is more important than individual adult sexual satisfaction threatens the family stability and endurance so critical to raising well-adjusted children.

Since same-sex marriage began in Scandinavia, family formation, stability, and endurance have all gotten much worse. Not only have few same-sex couples actually married since it became legal, but the change has weakened marriage and family commitments throughout society. Already high rates of family dissolution and non-married parenting have shot up, and the rate has dropped at which anyone is getting married at all.

EVALUATING THE AUTHORS' ARGUMENTS:

Daniel R. Heimbach claims that the love gay couples feel for one another is not enough to justify including them in the institution of marriage. How do you think Lester Olson, author of the previous viewpoint, would respond to this claim? With which author do you agree? Use evidence from the text to support your answer.

Legalized Gay Marriage Is Inevitable

Bernard Whitman

"No matter your opinion on the subject, this truth is inexorable: Gays and lesbians will one day be able to wed legally in all 50 states."

In the following viewpoint Bernard Whitman explains why he thinks gay marriage will eventually be legalized everywhere in America. The gay rights movement has already made tremendous progress more quickly than both supporters and opponents ever dreamed. Whitman says that homosexuality is now mainstream—this is not because there are more gays than before but because society is more accepting and acknowledging of them. Young people particularly favor gay marriage, he says, and even conservative arguments against gay marriage are faltering. Conservatives frequently support small government and social policy that is good for the economy, and Whitman says that gay marriage is about keeping the government out of private lives and will also stimulate business. For all these reasons, Whitman says that before long, gay marriage will be legal everywhere in the United States.

Whitman is president and CEO of Whitman Insight Strategies, a public opinion polling firm. He has appeared as a commentator on MSNBC, CNN, and Fox News.

AS YOU READ, CONSIDER THE FOLLOWING QUESTIONS:
1. What comparison does the author make between gay Americans and women and blacks?
2. How many Americans say they know someone who is gay, according to the author? How many have a gay friend, colleague, or family member?
3. What percent of Americans aged eighteen to thirty-four does Whitman say support gay marriage?

M arriage equality is going to happen in this country. It's only a matter of time.

For some, this reality is exciting, uplifting and extraordinary. For others, it is scary, frightening, even unfathomable. But no matter your opinion on the subject, this truth is inexorable: Gays and lesbians will one day be able to wed legally in all 50 states. Our relationships will finally be recognized as valid under the law and protected by our government. And America will be a stronger country for it.

How did we get here? And how did this happen so quickly? Change is not easy and usually takes much time, particularly a shift as dramatic as this one. But the fight for marriage equality has been particularly quick.

A generation ago, few thought it possible that gays and lesbians would ever be able to get married. When my good friend Evan Wolfson, the "godfather" of marriage equality, began arguing his case 20 years ago, most LGBT leaders privately said, "Evan, you're a great guy, but enough with this marriage stuff, it's never going to happen, and you're hurting the movement." Fortunately, he and others kept pressing forward, and in just a few months, marriage equality will be legal in at least four states—including Iowa, in the heartland of America.

Why is the freedom to marry so important? For starters, marriage is the most universally recognized social institution in the world. So if the ultimate goal is to achieve full equality for gays and lesbians in all aspects of society, then achieving equality in this most prominent arena will certainly go far toward realizing this vision. More

According to Fivethirtyeight.com, a Web site that makes political predictions based on statistical data, gay marriage will be legal in all states by 2024. They made these calculations factoring in the history of gay marriage amendments, public opinion tracking surveys, and the percentage of white evangelicals in a state.

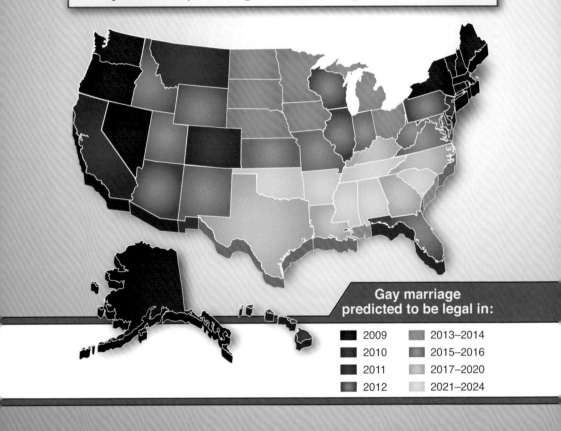

Gay marriage predicted to be legal in:

2009	2013–2014
2010	2015–2016
2011	2017–2020
2012	2021–2024

Taken from: Nate Silver, Fivethirtyeight, April 3, 2009. www.fivethirtyeight.com.

important, marriage is, at its core, a public recognition of a private commitment that two people in love make to each other, a commitment that transcends gender.

At the end of the day, all gays and lesbians—and their many straight allies—are looking for is basic respect for themselves as human beings, equal to any other human being, no more and no less.

Is that such an unreasonable request? After all, this country was founded on the promise that all men are created equal, with certain unalienable rights, including life, liberty and the pursuit of happiness. Along the way, this great country of ours has had to make changes to ensure that everyone can realize this American dream—most notably, ensuring that blacks and women are afforded the same rights and privileges as everyone else. And now America is realizing the same needs to be done for gays and lesbians, a group that some argue is the last one many believe it is acceptable to discriminate against.

The explanation for such a dramatic shift is actually quite simple: Americans began to come out—in droves. Suddenly, it seemed, gays and lesbians were everywhere: friends, family members, co-workers, characters on TV and in the movies, celebrities. Seven in 10 Americans know someone who is gay, and nearly half say they have a gay friend, colleague or family member, up from less than 40% only a decade ago.

Of course, the number of gay people hasn't changed, it's just that people started living openly and being honest with others about their sexual orientation. As soon as "mainstream" America started realizing just how many gay people they knew, Americans became much more accepting.

But still, isn't it a big cultural leap from accepting gays and lesbians in general to supporting the freedom to marry? Actually, no. The primary reason cited for opposition to marriage is religion. But marriage equality isn't about religion at all. Marriage equality is a civil rights issue.

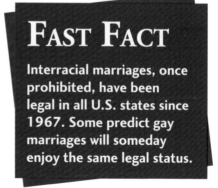

FAST FACT

Interracial marriages, once prohibited, have been legal in all U.S. states since 1967. Some predict gay marriages will someday enjoy the same legal status.

No one, not even the most ardent supporters of marriage, suggests that any particular religious institution be required to perform a wedding between two men or two women if that would go against that institution's religious teaching. After all, who would require Baptists to take communion, or Jews to accept Christ as their savior?

Religions have plenty of prohibitions against actions that are perfectly legal in our society, including working on the Sabbath, eating shellfish, drinking alcohol or coffee or celebrating Halloween. Would anyone think to suggest that these activities be prevented *by law* simply because some people's religions are opposed? Of course not.

What many people tend to forget is that marriage in our society is a legal contract between two individuals that is sanctioned by the state. Couples may choose to celebrate their wedding in a church, synagogue or mosque, and have a religious leader perform the ceremony, but in order for that marriage to be legal the officiant must be recognized by the state.

And while religions certainly have rules that married couples are supposed to follow, it is the state that decides who may get married and who may not, when marriages begin and end, and what rights, benefits and privileges are awarded to married people. There are currently over 1,100 rights, protections and responsibilities guaranteed to married couples by the federal government alone—rights that are denied to gay couples no matter how long they have been together.

Many people suggest that gays and lesbians should simply accept civil unions in the place of marriage. They argue that if it's just a matter of rights, we should create a separate institution that could serve as a vehicle to deliver the same benefits of marriage. And with more than two in three Americans supporting some form of legal status for gay couples, shouldn't we just accept civil unions, be grateful and move on? What's in a name, anyhow?

The truth is, everything. Marriage needs no explanation; everybody gets it. Most people have no idea what a civil union is, making it a terrible way to guarantee anything. The New Jersey Civil Union Review Commission concluded that civil unions have "not delivered equality to LGBT couples . . . a separate scheme does not create equality." The Supreme Courts of California and Connecticut came to the same conclusion, as did the Vermont State Legislature when last month it overrode the governor's veto to establish marriage equality, effective Sept. 1 of this year.

The problem with much of the discussion around marriage equality and civil unions is the false choice between marriage, civil unions or nothing at all. It allows many well-meaning individuals to avoid grappling with the M-word and still feel they are being supportive.

Former John McCain campaign chief strategist Steve Schmidt (pictured) speaks in favor of gay marriage.

But "separate but equal" never works. Didn't we learn that the hard way in the last century?

Particularly encouraging in the debate over marriage is the dramatic increase in support among young people. A majority (53%) of those aged 18 to 34 already support the freedom to marry—and in some states, like New York, that figure jumps to 71%. Nearly half of all adults nationwide now believe gays and lesbians should have the freedom to marry, almost double the figure recorded just a decade ago.

Not surprisingly, then, we are beginning to see significant cracks in the GOP's opposition. In his first public address since the election, John McCain's former chief strategist, Steve Schmidt, spoke out forcefully in favor of marriage at the Log Cabin Republican convention, warning his party that "if you put public policy issues to a religious test you risk becoming a religious party, and in a free country a political party cannot remain viable in the long term if it is seen as sectarian."

Meghan McCain, speaking at the same gathering, was equally clear: "I am a pro-life, pro-gay marriage Republican. So if anyone is still confused, let me spell it out for you: I believe life begins at conception, and I believe that people who fall in love should have the option to get married."

I'm delighted to hear conservatives step up on this issue, as I've always found it strange that the party of limited government and personal responsibility is opposed to marriage. It's been said that Republicans want government small enough to fit in your bedroom. Perhaps this sentiment is beginning to change.

And with good reason. I was recently on Fox News, and during the break asked my fellow guests—all prominent conservatives—how they justify denying gays and lesbians the freedom to marry when they agree that government should have less influence in our lives and that we need to do all we can to strengthen our families and communities.

I was met by stunned silence. The reality is that the freedom to marry is entirely consistent with the fundamentals of the Republican Party. Last time I checked, allowing two men or two women to marry will only strengthen the free market. They've got to buy a cake, right?

What we need now is leadership, and that needs to come from Democrats too. The party that says it stands for gay and lesbian equality must support the freedom to marry. While a handful of senators and representatives support marriage, including the Speaker of the House, we need far more of our national leaders to step up—including President Obama, who was himself the son of a marriage that was illegal in 22 states when he was born. He did leave the door ajar, writing in *The Audacity of Hope* that I "remain open to the possibility that my unwillingness to support gay marriage is misguided. . . . I may have been infected with society's prejudices . . . and that in years hence I may be seen as someone who was on the wrong side of history."

I always found it interesting that the first presidential candidate I ever heard come out in favor of the freedom to marry was the Rev. Al Sharpton, who said that asking him "if he was in favor of gay marriage was like asking if he was in favor of white marriage or black marriage."

As a pollster, I'm well aware of the political danger of getting out in front of public opinion. But sometimes leadership demands as much. The truth is, we should never put people's civil rights up for a vote. Our constitution was designed to protect the minority from the tyranny of the majority.

At the end of the day, marriage equality will come: partly through the courts; partly through the legislative process. More and more community and political leaders will offer their support, and someday soon gays and lesbians all across America will be able to choose to get married, or not.

Which side of this history do you want to be on?

EVALUATING THE AUTHORS' ARGUMENTS:

In Bernard Whitman's opinion, the legality of gay marriage is inevitable, as was the right of women and African Americans to vote. Write two or three sentences on how you think each author in this chapter would respond to this argument. Then, state whether you agree and why.

Legalized Gay Marriage Is Not Inevitable

"[Carrie Prejean] gave permission to conservative cultural elites to talk about [gay marriage]— and so gave ordinary Americans permission to tell pollsters what they really think."

Maggie Gallagher

Legalized gay marriage is by no means inevitable, argues Maggie Gallagher in the following viewpoint. She says it simply appears that way because conservative Americans, politicians, and commentators have become afraid to speak out against it. She says that gay marriage advocates have unfairly painted those who oppose gay marriage as bigots and have used scare tactics to silence them. But in reality, the majority of the country opposes gay marriage, as was revealed when a young beauty queen named Carrie Prejean innocently stated her support for traditional marriage and unleashed a tidal wave of public opposition to it. Gallagher urges those who oppose gay marriage not to be afraid to stand up and be counted. When they are, she says, it will become clear that legalized gay marriage will never become a reality.

Gallagher is the president of National Organization for Marriage, an organization that opposes same-sex marriage.

Maggie Gallagher, "The Carrie Effect: Notes from the Frontlines of the Marriage War," Coalition for Marriage and Family, July 31, 2009. Reproduced by permission of the author.

The headline on the story about a new CBS News/*New York Times* survey was interesting: "Poll: Support for Gay Marriage Dips." How fast and how far had support for gay marriage had to drop before a mainstream-media headline acknowledged it, even as a "dip"?

Here's the answer: 9 percentage points.

That's right: In just a few short months, support for gay marriage in this poll plunged 9 percentage points, from its all-time high of 42 percent to 33 percent.

Resistance to Gay Marriage Is Not Futile

A reporter for *New York* magazine recently called me to ask about the cause of a similar abrupt drop in support for gay marriage in a poll of voters in New York State. "Did the National Organization for Marriage [NOM]"—of which I am president—"cause that decline?" he asked. I suspect he wanted me to claim credit, to give him a more dramatic narrative. After all, if you run a large activist organization directly involved in politics, your professional obligation is to be a blowhard. (And indeed, the 2 million robocalls and the ad campaign NOM had launched must have helped.) But I turned in my professional-blowhard card by saying, "No, I really think that it was [Miss California] Carrie Prejean."

The Carrie Effect? How can one beauty queen cause a swing of almost ten points in national polls on a hotly debated issue?

Culture consists of ideas. Ideas, like civilizations, can die out. They die when no one is willing to defend them out loud. Gay-marriage advocates are like the [*Star Trek*] Borg: Resistance is futile, they repeatedly say. This is an ambitious and psychologically sophisticated strategy: If they say it often enough, maybe Americans will believe it. If Americans start to believe it, then it will be true. Despair is gay-marriage advocates' most powerful weapon, especially when it is fed by social conservatives' failure to create solid strategies of hope. . . .

Politicians and Commentators Are Afraid to Speak Their Minds

Why don't *politicians* speak out more often? After all, nearly 60 percent of Americans are on our side. The answer: Politicians even in conservative parts of the country do not want to speak out, because they do not want to be targeted by [aggressive gay marriage advocates]. Thus has another whole category of symbolic analysts been silenced.

Silencing the opposition is also at the heart of a new tactic that emerged in the wake of Prop 8[1] going after donors to California's marriage amendment, whose names and addresses are publicly disclosed by law. One woman e-mailed me recently. She had given a few hundred dollars to the pro-Prop 8 effort. Her home address was put on an Internet site, and she continues to receive angry, nasty, sometimes vile letters from strangers. "Should I be afraid to go outside my door?" she asked. Probably not, I tell her, But most Americans aren't used to the idea that peacefully participating in democratic processes requires any degree of physical courage. . . .

Meanwhile, conservative talk radio and television is almost silent on the gay-marriage issue, with the exception of some explicitly Christian shows. Why? I cannot tell you. I *can* tell you that I was recently invited (by a substitute host) to appear on a major conservative talk program. The producer came into the room just before we went on the air to offer (nervously) some instructions: "We don't talk about gay marriage directly on this show. We talk about the religious-liberty side, but not gay marriage." Deep in the red heart of America, in the control room of a major conservative talk-radio show, people are afraid to speak against gay marriage.

1. A 2008 California ballot initiative that overturned gay marriage in that state.

An Honest Answer Changes Everything

And at precisely this moment, as a few legislatures began to pass gay marriage and a handful of Republicans ostentatiously began to endorse it, as gay-marriage advocates tried to break the back of the opposition by demonstrating that the debate was over, along came Carrie Prejean.

A stunning young Christian beauty-pageant contestant was asked on national television by a gay celebrity blogger (whatever that is) what she thought about gay marriage. Watch the video clip on YouTube. You can see in her eyes that she knows: If she says what she thinks, she is not going to be Miss USA. She's 21 years old. She's worked very, very hard for that tiara. She comes from a modest family background. Money is tight, especially since she had to quit her job to prepare for the pageant.

The tiara means a luxury apartment. It means the possibility of a lucrative modeling career. You can see in her eyes that she realizes all she has to do is . . . fudge. "I don't like to watch that video," Carrie has told me. She doesn't like it for the very reason I found it

A storm of controversy arose when beauty pageant contestant Carrie Prejean, Miss California (pictured), made statements opposing gay marriage.

so powerfully moving: In the space of 30 seconds, you see a young woman first be tempted and then decide that no, she cannot fudge, she has to tell the truth. "I believe that a marriage should be between a man and a woman. No offense to anybody out there." You see her choose between truth and the tiara. She never asked for this ordeal, but she was tested and she triumphed. . . .

Do Not Be Afraid to Oppose Gay Marriage

The romance, the moral drama, unfolding on national TV captured Americans' attention. All of a sudden, opposition to gay marriage was all over radio and TV. The new face of opposition to gay marriage was a young, beautiful woman who did nothing other than answer a question honestly in a beauty pageant—and the hatred unleashed against her made the current strategy of the gay-marriage movement highly visible. [Internet celebrity gossip columnist] Perez Hilton's angry, expletive-packed diatribe reminded too many people of what they saw after Prop 8. Most important, Carrie singlehandedly ended the virtual news blackout on gay marriage in Vermont, Maine, and New Hampshire, and trumped the media's attempt to portray public response to developments there as muted.

FAST FACT

Since Massachusetts became the first state to legalize gay marriage in 2003, just five other states have followed suit.

She gave permission to conservative cultural elites to talk about the issue—and so gave ordinary Americans permission to tell pollsters what they really think.

The Country Does Not Want Gay Marriage

Gay marriage did not start passing legislatures as the result of a sudden wave of populist sentiment for it. Public sentiment has not shifted one bit toward gay marriage since last November [2008], when voters in a blue state (California), a purple state (Florida), and a red state (Arizona) once again affirmed that the majority of Americans oppose it.

A Gallup poll released in late May [2009] demonstrates the surprising stability of opposition to gay marriage: "Americans' views on same-sex marriage have essentially stayed the same in the past year":

57 percent opposed, 40 percent in favor. "Though support for legal same-sex marriage is significantly higher now than when Gallup first asked about it in 1996, in recent years support has appeared to stall." Gallup asked voters whether gay marriage would make the country better off, make it worse off, or make no difference. Only 13 percent of Americans said gay marriage would help the country; 48 percent said it would make the country worse off.

Even in Massachusetts, six years after courts imposed gay marriage, public opposition remains surprisingly high. In a poll of Massachusetts voters taken in late March [2009] by the National Organization for Marriage and the Massachusetts Family Institute, respondents narrowly opposed it, 44 percent to 43 percent.

Other polls confirm the stability of Americans' views on marriage. In an April 2009 Pew poll, even a plurality of 18- to 29-year-olds—the most pro-gay-marriage age group—opposed it, by a margin of 45 percent to 43 percent.

Do Not Be Fooled: Gay Marriage Is Not Inevitable

There is a generation gap on gay marriage, but the biggest gap is between cultural elites and everyone else. The urgent job facing marriage advocates is to take an issue on which we have the agreement of almost 60 percent of the American people and translate that into politically effective organizations that can elect our friends and defeat our enemies. If we continue to fail to do so, our political opponents will use their cultural power to create an America in which traditional religious groups are redefined by the government as the moral and legal equivalent of racists.

That was the point of the strange public outburst of hatred that ensued when Carrie Prejean said, "I believe that a marriage should be between a man and a woman." Gay-marriage advocates understand that if you can persuade elites that gay marriage is inevitable, public opinion won't matter, because it will be silent. An idea that people are afraid to speak ceases to matter.

That is their best hope, and our opportunity.

EVALUATING THE AUTHOR'S ARGUMENTS:

Maggie Gallagher argues that public support for gay marriage is an illusion. Explain what she means by this. Do you agree with her? Why or why not? Use evidence from the texts you have read to support your answer.

Chapter 2

What Effect Would Legalized Gay Marriage Have?

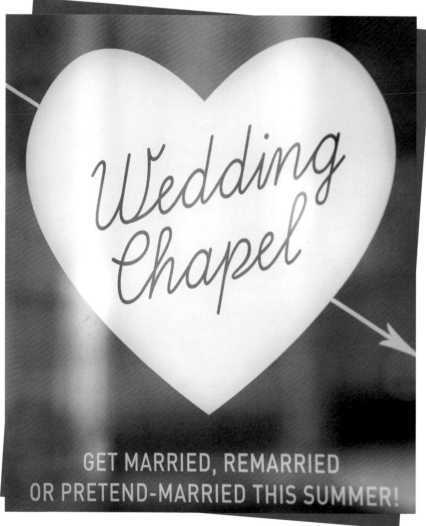

GET MARRIED, REMARRIED
OR PRETEND-MARRIED THIS SUMMER!

*A wedding chapel in New York performs
unofficial gay marriages despite the state's ban
on such unions.*

Marriage Would Strengthen Gay Relationships

Jacob Gershman

"Granting legal recognition to these relationships can only strengthen . . . families, by extending the ability to participate in this crucial social institution. . . ."

In the following viewpoint, Jacob Gershman discusses ex–New York governor Eliot Spitzer's argument to legalize same-sex marriage. Spitzer directly confronts the opposition's belief that gay marriage would erode the institution of marriage. He states that same-sex couples wish to marry in order to have a binding obligation to one another and to share in a life of intimacy with emotional support. The legal recognition of these relationships would strengthen families, not tear them apart.

Jacob Gershman is a staff reporter for the *New York Sun*.

AS YOU READ, CONSIDER THE FOLLOWING QUESTIONS:

1. As stated in the article in a historical context, why should New York State approve a bill legalizing gay marriage?
2. How many votes would the bill need in the Assembly in order to pass the chamber?
3. If signed into law, what would Spitzer's bill do for New York?

Jacob Gershman, "Gay Rites Will Help Families, Spitzer Says," *New York Sun,* May 8, 2007. Reproduced by permission.

L egalizing gay marriage would "only strengthen New York's families," according to [ex–New York] Governor [Eliot] Spitzer, who laid forth his most detailed argument in favor of recognizing same-sex relationships in a legislative memo.

Mr. Spitzer, who late last month [April 2007] became the nation's first governor to propose legislation legalizing gay marriage, articulated a legal and moral argument in defense of the bill in a two-page "statement in support" that is being distributed to lawmakers.

The governor's forceful language adds even more contrast between his position and that of the major Democratic candidates for president, including [then-]Senator [Hillary] Clinton, all of whom oppose gay marriage but favor civil unions.

Supporters of the bill said they were heartened and surprised by the governor's appeal and said they viewed it as another sign that gay marriage could become a more mainstream Democratic position. While Mr. Spitzer's stance is not shared by his party's top-tier White House hopefuls, it could become a more widely accepted position within the party by 2012, when Mr. Spitzer, a nationally known political figure, may be a candidate for president.

Gay Marriage Does Not Erode the Institution

The memo, which was prepared by the governor's counsel, directly confronts one of the main arguments made by opponents of gay marriage, who have warned that allowing same-sex couples to marry would erode the institution of marriage.

"Same-sex couples who wish to marry are not simply looking to obtain additional rights, they are seeking out substantial responsibilities as well: to undertake significant and binding obligations to one another, and to lives of 'shared intimacy and mutual financial and emotional support,'" the memo states.

"Granting legal recognition to these relationships can only strengthen New York's families, by extending the ability to participate in this crucial social institution to all New Yorkers."

Opponents of gay marriage said the governor was trying to co-opt their argument.

The author discusses ex–New York governor Eliot Spitzer's support of gay marriage, which would allow people like this couple to wed. According to Spitzer, gay marriage would strengthen families.

"He's couching it in this family values language, which is insulting. He's trying to turn our argument on its head," a spokesman for the New York State Catholic Conference, Dennis Poust, said. The conference is the public policy arm of the bishops of New York.

"He's taking a radical turn, and he's going to alienate a lot of people," Mr. Poust said.

Civil Unions Are Insufficient

The bill memo also suggests that civil unions, adopted by a number of states to confer many of the legal rights enjoyed by married couples, offer insufficient protection.

"Civil marriage is the means by which the state defines a couple's place in society. Those who are excluded from its rubric are told by the institutions of the State, in essence, that their solemn commitment to one another has no legal weight," the memo says.

Mr. Spitzer also tries to place the legislation in a historical context by arguing that the "history of this country" has been a story

> **FAST FACT**
>
> According to the U.S. Census Bureau, about 100,000 official same-sex weddings, civil unions, and domestic partnerships took place or were registered in 2008.

of excluded groups achieving access to equal rights. New York has long been a main character in that story, the memo says.

"New York State, in particular, has played a proud and honorable part in that history, from hosting the foundational women's rights convention at Seneca Falls in 1848, to breaking baseball's color barrier, to witnessing the seminal event of the modern gay rights movement in New York City almost four decades ago," the memo says.

Mr. Spitzer, who said during his campaign [in 2006] that he would seek to legalize gay marriage, released the bill without a press conference and was out of state last week when gay rights groups came to Albany for a day of lobbying.

Last month, when he talked to reporters about his legislative priorities, he did not raise the issue of gay marriage. His low-key approach suggested to some backers of gay marriage that the governor was more concerned about making good on a campaign promise than he was in shepherding the bill through the Legislature.

All Families Deserve Protection

Assemblyman Daniel O'Donnell, an openly gay lawmaker from Manhattan who is sponsoring the governor's bill in the Assembly,

Gay Marriage Around the World

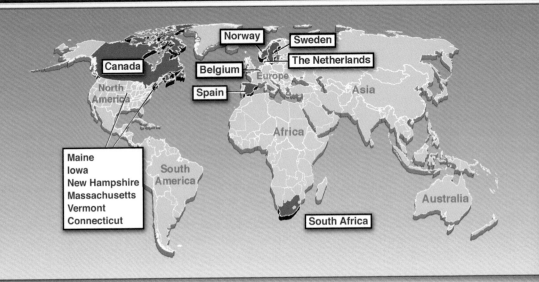

As of 2009 same-sex marriage was legal in seven countries and a handful of U.S. states.

Norway

Sweden

Canada

Belgium

The Netherlands

Europe

North America

Spain

Asia

Africa

Maine
Iowa
New Hampshire
Massachusetts
Vermont
Connecticut

South America

Australia

South Africa

Taken from: ILGA, the International Lesbian, Gay, Bisexual, Trans and Intersex Association, May 2009.

said the memo "shows that he has an emotional and intellectual commitment to providing equality to all New Yorkers."

He said, "We have language that tells the ultimate truth. We are part of the American family. We have people who are part of families and our families deserve as much protection as all other families."

Mr. Spitzer has said he doubts that the Legislature would pass the bill this year. Gay rights activists have a short-term goal of passage in the Democrat-controlled Assembly, where support for gay marriage is stronger than it is in the Republican-controlled Senate.

The Assembly speaker, Sheldon Silver, has not taken a position on the governor's bill, which would need at least 76 votes out of 150 in the Assembly to pass the chamber. A similar gay marriage bill introduced in the Assembly this year had more than 40 sponsors.

If signed into law, New York would be the first state in the nation to legalize gay marriage through a legislative process and the second state in the nation—after Massachusetts—to extend marriage to same-sex couples.

EVALUATING THE AUTHORS' ARGUMENTS:

Jacob Gershman and the author of the next viewpoint, Sam Schulman, disagree on whether marriage can benefit gay couples. After reading both viewpoints, with which author do you agree? What pieces of evidence swayed you?

Marriage Would Not Enhance Gay Relationships

Sam Schulman

"*Gay couples who marry are bound to be disappointed in marriage's impotence.*"

In the following viewpoint Sam Schulman explains why he believes gay couples have no use for marriage. He says that at heart, marriage is about more than just loving a partner. Society created marriage for a few key purposes: to protect a woman's virtue and virginity; to make sure no children were born from incestuous or interfaith relationships; and to make sex sociably acceptable. But Schulman says that by their very nature, gay relationships have no need for any of these aspects of marriage. Gay people do not lose their virginity; no children can be born from any gay union; and out-of-wedlock gay sex is already viewed as acceptable. Schulman predicts that once gay couples realize that marriage does not offer them anything they do not already have, they will lose interest in obtaining it.

Schulman is a writer whose articles have appeared in the *New York Press*, the *Spectator*, and the *Weekly Standard*, from which this viewpoint was taken.

Sam Schulman, "The Worst Thing About Gay Marriage: It Isn't Going to Work," *Weekly Standard*, vol. 14, June 1, 2009. Copyright © 2009, News Corporation, Weekly Standard. All rights reserved. Reproduced by permission.

The relationship between a same-sex couple, though it involves the enviable joy of living forever with one's soulmate, loyalty, fidelity, warmth, a happy home, shopping, and parenting, is not the same as marriage between a man and a woman, though they enjoy exactly the same cozy virtues. These qualities are awfully nice, but they are emphatically not what marriage fosters, and, even when they do exist, are only a small part of why marriage evolved and what it does.

The entity known as "gay marriage" only aspires to replicate a very limited, very modern, and very culture-bound version of marriage. Gay advocates have chosen wisely in this. They are replicating what we might call the "romantic marriage," a kind of marriage that is chosen, determined, and defined by the couple that enters into it. Romantic marriage is now dominant in the West and is becoming slightly more frequent in other parts of the world. But it is a luxury and even here has only existed (except among a few elites) for a couple of centuries—and in only a few countries. The fact is that marriage is part of a much larger institution, which defines the particular shape and character of marriage: the kinship system.

Marriage Is Part of the Kinship System

The role that marriage plays in kinship encompasses far more than arranging a happy home in which two hearts may beat as one—in fact marriage is actually pretty indifferent to that particular aim. Nor has marriage historically concerned itself with compelling the particular male and female who have created a child to live together and care for that child. It is not the "right to marry" that creates an enduring relationship between heterosexual lovers or a stable home for a child, but the more far-reaching kinship system that assigns every one of the vast array of marriage rules a set of duties and obligations to enforce. These duties and obligations impinge even on romantic marriage, and not always to its advantage. The obligations of kinship imposed on traditional marriage have nothing to do with the romantic ideals expressed in gay marriage.

Consider four of the most profound effects of marriage within the kinship system.

Marriage Is for Protecting Female Sexuality

The first is the most important: It is that marriage is concerned above all with female sexuality. The very existence of kinship depends on the protection of females from rape, degradation, and concubinage. This is why marriage between men and women has been necessary in virtually every society ever known. Marriage, whatever its particular

The author claims that gays should not marry because marriage was originally intended to protect a woman's virtue.

manifestation in a particular culture or epoch, is essentially about who may and who may not have sexual access to a woman when she becomes an adult, and is also about how her adulthood—and sexual accessibility—is defined. . . .

This most profound aspect of marriage—protecting and controlling the sexuality of the child-bearing sex—is its only true reason for being, and it has no equivalent in same-sex marriage. Virginity until marriage, arranged marriages, the special status of the sexuality of one partner but not the other (and her protection from the other sex)—these motivating forces for marriage do not apply to same-sex lovers.

No Need to Ban Incest or Interfaith Unions in Gay Relationships

Second, kinship modifies marriage by imposing a set of rules that determines not only whom one may marry (someone from the right clan or family, of the right age, with proper abilities, wealth, or an adjoining vineyard), but, more important, whom one may not marry. Incest prohibition and other kinship rules that dictate one's few permissible and many impermissible sweethearts are part of traditional marriage. Gay marriage is blissfully free of these constraints. There is no particular reason to ban sexual intercourse between brothers, a father and a son of consenting age, or mother and daughter.

There are no questions of ritual pollution: Will a hip Rabbi refuse to marry a Jewish man—even a Cohen—to a Gentile man? Do Irish women avoid Italian women? A same-sex marriage fails utterly to create forbidden relationships. If Tommy marries Bill, and they divorce, and Bill later marries a woman and has a daughter, no incest prohibition prevents Bill's daughter from marrying Tommy. The relationship between Bill and Tommy is a romantic fact, but it can't be fitted into the kinship system.

No Need to Legitimize Gay Sex with Marriage

Third, marriage changes the nature of sexual relations between a man and a woman. Sexual intercourse between a married couple is licit [lawful]; sexual intercourse before marriage, or adulterous sex during marriage, is not. . . .

Now to live in such a system, in which sexual intercourse can be illicit, is a great nuisance. Many of us feel that licit sexuality loses, moreover, a bit of its oomph. Gay lovers live merrily free of this system. Can we imagine Frank's family and friends warning him that "if Joe were serious, he would put a ring on your finger"? Do we ask Vera to stop stringing Sally along? Gay sexual practice is not sortable into these categories—licit-if-married but illicit-if-not (children adopted by a gay man or hygienically conceived by a lesbian mom can never be regarded as illegitimate). Neither does gay copulation become in any way more permissible, more noble after marriage. It is a scandal that homosexual intercourse should ever have been illegal, but having become legal, there remains no extra sanction—the kind which fathers with shotguns enforce upon heterosexual lovers. I am not aware of any gay marriage activist who suggests that gay men and women should create a new category of disapproval for their own sexual relationships, after so recently having been freed from the onerous and bigoted legal blight on homosexual acts. But without social disapproval of unmarried sex—what kind of madman would seek marriage? . . .

FAST FACT

According to the Institute for Marriage and Public Policy, only 1 to 5 percent of gays and lesbians take advantage of same-sex marriage in countries where it is legal.

Gay Couples Have No Use for "Marriage"

None of these facts apply at all to love between people of the same sex, however solemn and profound that love may be. In gay marriage there are no virgins (actual or honorary), no incest, no illicit or licit sex, no merging of families, no creation of a new lineage. There's just my honey and me, and (in a rapidly increasing number of U.S. states) baby makes three. . . .

Sooner rather than later, the substantial differences between marriage and gay marriage will cause gay marriage, as a meaningful and popular institution, to fail on its own terms. Since gay relationships

Gay Relationships Are Not as Strong as Straight Ones

Studies, surveys, and census data show that heterosexual relationships last longer than homosexual ones.

Percent of Heterosexual Marriages Remaining Intact (by length of marriage)

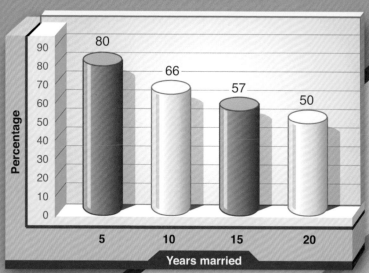

Length of Current Homosexual Relationship (years to date)

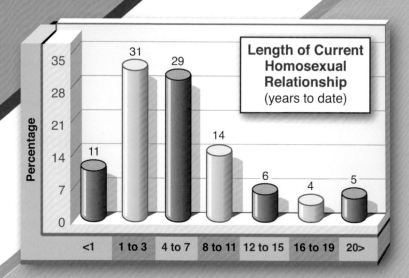

Taken from: Family Research Council, "Comparing the Lifestyle of Homosexual Couples to Married Couples", 2005.

exist perfectly well outside the kinship system, to assume the burdens of marriage—the legal formalities, the duty of fidelity (which is no easier for gays than it is for straights), the slavishly imitative wedding ritual—will come to seem a nuisance. People in gay marriages will discover that mimicking the cozy bits of romantic heterosexual marriage does not make relationships stronger; romantic partners more loving, faithful, or sexy; domestic life more serene or exciting. They will discover that it is not the wedding vow that maintains marriages, but the force of the kinship system. Kinship imposes duties, penalties, and retribution that champagne toasts, self-designed wedding rings, and thousands of dollars worth of flowers are powerless to effect.

Gay Marriage Would Be a Letdown

Few men would ever bother to enter into a romantic heterosexual marriage—much less three, as I have done—were it not for the iron grip of necessity that falls upon us when we are unwise enough to fall in love with a woman other than our mom. There would be very few flowerings of domestic ecstasy were it not for the granite underpinnings of marriage. Gay couples who marry are bound to be disappointed in marriage's impotence without these ghosts of past authority. Marriage has a lineage more ancient than any divine revelation, and before any system of law existed, kinship crushed our ancestors with complex and pitiless roles about incest, family, tribe, and totem. Gay marriage, which can be created by any passel [large number] of state supreme court justices with degrees from middling law schools, lacking the authority and majesty of the kinship system, will be a letdown.

When, in spite of current enthusiasm, gay marriage turns out to disappoint or bore the couples now so eager for its creation, its failure will be utterly irrelevant for gay people. The happiness of gay relationships up to now has had nothing to do with being married or unmarried; nor will they in the future. I suspect that the gay marriage movement will be remembered as a faintly humorous, even embarrassing stage in the liberation saga of the gay minority. The archetypal gay wedding portrait—a pair of middle-aged women or paunchy men looking uncomfortable in rented outfits worn at the wrong time of day—is destined to be hung in the same gallery of dated images of social progress alongside snapshots of flappers defiantly puffing cigarettes and Kodachromes of African Americans wearing dashikis [African garments]. The freedom of gays to live openly as they please will easily survive the death of gay marriage.

EVALUATING THE AUTHOR'S ARGUMENTS:

To make his argument, Sam Schulman explains that romantic marriage is just one part of the historical institution of marriage. Do you agree with him that marriage is for protecting virginity, avoiding incest and interfaith unions, and other reasons? Why or why not? Use specific examples from the text to make your argument.

Gay Marriage Strengthens the Institution of Marriage

Mike Alvear

"*[Gay marriages] will reduce divorces by preventing sham marriages. . . . It's one of those queer ironies: Gay marriage will strengthen heterosexual families.*"

Extending marriage rights to gay couples strengthens the institution of marriage, argues Mike Alvear in the following viewpoint. He says that all of society is hurt by homophobia, which he says is the main force preventing gays from legally marrying each other. In addition to hurting all of the family members and friends of gay people, homophobia forces gay people to hide their sexuality. As a result, they enter into sham marriages that are doomed to divorce. Alvear says if gay marriage were legal, such marriages could be avoided. In addition, legalized gay marriage strengthens neighborhoods and families, both of which are good for society. Alvear concludes that admitting more committed, loving couples to the marriage club only helps strengthen the institution.

Alvear is a columnist for the political Web site The Huffington Post.

Mike Alvear, "Gay Marriage: How It Strengthens Heterosexual Marriages," Mike Alvear's Urge & Merge, April 3, 2009. www.mikealvear.com. Reproduced by permission.

AS YOU READ, CONSIDER THE FOLLOWING QUESTIONS:
1. What is a "fig leaf marriage," as described by the author?
2. How many people does the author figure are directly or indirectly affected by homophobia? What percentage of these are straight people?
3. How can gay marriage help revitalize neighborhoods, in Alvear's opinion?

G ay marriage will reduce the number of divorces caused by fraudulent marriages, ensure that more orphaned children grow up in stable homes, raise the standard of living for children with gay parents, make neighborhoods safer for families, and boost the economies of struggling communities.

It's not the license to marry that will create these benefits; it's the massive shift in attitude that'll result from it. The more gays are accepted as equal citizens the more stable heterosexual marriage will become. Why? Because there are an untold number of "traditional" marriages that break up because one of the spouses comes out.

Gay Marriage Will Reduce the Number of Straight Divorces

Homophobia drives fearful gay men and women into fraudulent marriages. The pressure to conform, the weight of discrimination, the potential loss of cherished dreams (serving in the military, worshipping in church, getting job promotions, raising kids) propels many into marriages they otherwise wouldn't commit to. Like my friend Cooper.

Cooper is 64 and recently divorced. He was married for 38 years before he came out. He left behind him a woman whose life was shattered by a truth that tunneled its way out of the mounds of shame, hostility and hatred that society heaped on it. The woman is 62. What is she supposed to do with her life now that he's found his?

Homophobia has a way of wounding gay and straight alike. It creates two classes of victims: People who are forced to lie and the people they lie to. As homophobia decreases, so will the pressure for gays and lesbians to enter into fig leaf marriages. Which in turn, prevents children from being hurt by divorce and helps heterosexuals, like Cooper's wife, create authentic, stable marriages.

Homophobia Punishes Heterosexuals, Too

For every gay man and woman that gets punished by the legal system there are straight mothers and fathers and brothers and sisters who suffer with them.

According to my calculations, 57.6 million people are either directly or indirectly affected by homophobia. Since demographers believe there are only about 6.4 million self-identified gay people, that means 89% of the people affected by discrimination against gays are heterosexual.

Estimated Numbers:

6.4 million gays and lesbians

6.4 million siblings of gays and lesbians (assuming each gay person has one sibling)

12.8 million parents of gays and lesbians (assuming each parent is alive)

25.6 million grandparents (assuming two sets of living grandparents)

6.4 million uncles and aunts (assuming one per gay person)

Total: 57.6 million

No matter how they feel about homosexuality, no parent wants to see their children hurt, no brother wants to see his sister in danger, no uncle wants to see his nephew suffer. One of the intangible costs of homophobia is the excruciating emotional pain felt by everyone related to the gay family member. Lessen homophobia, as gay marriage will, and you lessen the strain on millions of families.

How Gay Marriage Helps Your Neighborhood

Ferndale, Michigan's downtown was once lined with abandoned buildings. After years of courting gays to live and start businesses, it had a vacancy rate of less than 3 percent (before the recession hit).

Ferndale followed the theories in the bestselling book, *The Rise of the Creative Class.* Civic leaders across the country pay over $10,000 to hear the author, urban planner Richard Florida, talk about the best way to revitalize their communities. His thesis: If cities want to jump-start their economies they must attract the dominant economic group in America—people who think for a living (doctors, lawyers, scientists, engineers, entrepreneurs and computer programmers).

Dubbing them the "Creative Class," Florida points out they're the most dominant economic group, making up nearly 30% of the workforce.

Florida produced a number of indexes measuring characteristics of successful cities. There's a High-Tech Index (ranking cities by the size of their software, electronics and engineering sectors) and an Innovation Index (ranking cities by the number of patents per capita).

FAST FACT

A 2009 Quinnipiac University poll found that the majority of Americans—58 percent—believe same-sex marriages would not threaten traditional heterosexual marriages.

But one of Florida's most talked-about rankings is the Gay Index. He told Salon.com: "Gays are the canaries of the creative economy. Where gays are will be a community that has the underlying preconditions that attract the creative class of people. Gays tend to gravitate toward the types of places that will be attractive to many members of the creative class."

Florida, a professor at Carnegie Mellon University in Pittsburgh, boils it down to this: If you want economic growth one of the things you must do is attract gays. Not because there are disproportionate numbers of gays in "Thinking Jobs" but because their presence signals the values the creative class are attracted to: Diversity, open-mindedness, variety, eccentricity.

Examples of Florida's theories: Minneapolis's Loring Park, Boston's Jamaica Plain, Chicago's Boystown, Atlanta's Midtown, Washington's Dupont Circle and Adams-Morgan. Though each have the reputation of being "gay meccas," any demographer will tell you that the vast majority of residents are heterosexual.

Married Gay Couples Can Help Orphans

There are too many kids in foster care and not enough parents to adopt them. There are plenty of gay and lesbian families willing to adopt some of the 568,000 kids languishing in institutions, but statutory bans and local judiciaries refusing to grant gay adoption petitions impede them. According to the Evan B. Donaldson Adoption Institute's latest national survey, only 40% of public and private adoption agencies have placed children with gay adoptive parents. The same survey showed that a majority of childless gay men and women would like to become parents.

Would children in foster care be better off living in loving gay homes or institutions that warehouse and shuffle them from one home to another until they turn eighteen and "age out" of the system? Ask The American Academy of Pediatrics, The Child Welfare League of America, the North American Council on Adoptable Children, the American Psychiatric Association, the American Psychological Association, and the National Association of Social Workers. Their conclusion: Gay and lesbian homes.

What's the best way of making that happen? Giving gay couples automatic adoption rights. And the most effective way to do that? Allow them to marry.

Strengthen Families with Marriage

Gay marriage wouldn't just improve the lives of orphans; it would also improve the lives of children who have parents that happen to be gay.

Let's say two women with average incomes have a child together named Billy. Because the women aren't allowed to marry, Billy doesn't get the financial and emotional safety nets other kids get.

For example, if Billy has a serious accident while his biological mother is away, the hospital can deny him the right to see his second parent, effectively torturing the child at the time of his greatest need. If Billy comes home to recuperate, the boss isn't legally obligated to provide sick leave to Billy's second parent, effectively preventing a child from being soothed by his nurturing parent.

If Billy's biological mother dies, the surviving parent has no legal rights to Billy, effectively allowing the state to rip him from the arms of a loving mother and throw him into the foster care system. If Billy's parents separate, the departing parent is under no legal obligation to provide alimony or child support, effectively plunging Billy into poverty.

From his parents' inability to get joint health, home and auto insurance policies to his own inability to access his second parent's Social Security survival benefits, Billy suffers. Allowing same-sex marriage would eliminate the unfair penalties children have to bear. Ultimately, the greatest benefactors to gay marriage are children. Over half a million of them. . . .

Gay Marriage Is Good for America

Marriage, as everyone knows, is a stabilizing influence on relationships and a platform for greater prosperity. The benefits of marriage would encourage gays and lesbians to take even more risks in distressed neighborhoods, turning them into places that attract

The author argues that if gay marriage were legal, children of gay couples would find their lives greatly improved.

Gay Marriage Does Not Hurt Traditional Marriages

The majority of Americans do not think that legalized gay marriage would pose a threat to traditional marriage.

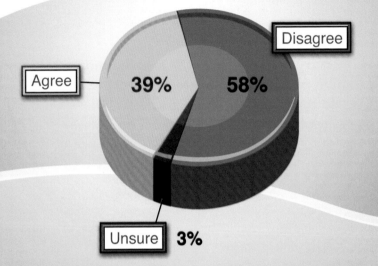

"Some people say that same-sex marriage is a threat to traditional marriage between a man and woman. Do you agree or disagree?"

Disagree

Agree

39%

58%

Unsure **3%**

Taken from: Quinnipiac University poll, April 21–27, 2009.

the mostly heterosexual "Creative Class." The payoff to cities is clear: Encouraging stability and prosperity among gay and lesbian couples results in a bigger tax base which can then be used to improve schools, streets, and parks for its mostly-heterosexual citizens.

The Iowa gay marriage [supreme court] opinion and its consequences won't just benefit same-sex couples; it will benefit everyone. It will reduce divorces by preventing sham marriages, provide homes to the orphaned, protect the children of gay parents and revitalize distressed communities. It's one of those queer ironies: Gay marriage will strengthen heterosexual families.

Gay Marriage Hurts the Institution of Marriage

David Benkof

"The gay and lesbian community barely understands marriage, particularly the part about fidelity."

In the following viewpoint David Benkof explains why he believes legalizing gay unions would hurt the institution of marriage. Benkof says that gays and straights hold very different attitudes about what constitutes a marriage. Traditionally, married people are loyal and committed to each other—and this means they have no extramarital physical or mental affairs. But Benkof says that having just one partner is not a common feature of gay relationships. He claims that gay people routinely have more than one sexual partner at a time when they are in a committed relationship, and even support open marriages (in which partners involve other people in their private sex lives). Benkof says that fidelity is a key component of the institution of marriage, and when gay couples fail to respect that element, they weaken the core of what marriage represents.

Benkof is a blogger at the site www.gays defendmarriage.com.

David Benkof, "Monogamous Same-Sex Adultery," SFGate.com, June 26, 2008. Reproduced by permission of the author.

AS YOU READ, CONSIDER THE FOLLOWING QUESTIONS:
1. What did the author *not* find when he did an Internet search for the words "marriage equality"?
2. What kinds of tips does Benkof say the gay marriage Web site Partners Task Force offers gay couples?
3. What does Benkof find telling about each of the four heterosexual politicians who most prominently support gay marriage?

I argue against same-sex marriage in part because I think the gay and lesbian community barely understands marriage, particularly the part about fidelity. Thus, I am accused of extrapolating the nonmonogamy of a few gay couples to an entire community, and reminded of the widespread cheating and swinging in the straight community.

But my concern is not about the extent of extramarital sex in each community. It's about the vast gulf in attitudes between gays and straights on whether a promise to be sexually exclusive is an essential component of a proper marriage.

Gay Couples Are Not Interested in Monogamy

A gay friend of mine, Los Angeles blogger Daniel Blatt, who believes in monogamy and sees the advantages to same-sex marriage, was taken aback when he searched on the words "marriage equality" and found very little mention of monogamy on Web sites promoting such. When I helped Blatt with his research, I stumbled upon a Web site hostile to monogamy that is promoted as a marriage resource by several major gay Web sites, including those of Marriage Equality USA, the Gay, Lesbian, and Straight Educators Network, Equality Texas, the Kentucky Fairness Alliance, and even the Metropolitan Community Church.

FAST FACT

A May 2008 Gallup Poll found that 56 percent of Americans believe same-sex marriages should not be recognized by law.

The Partners Task Force site, buddybuddy.com, does contain a few friendly words about monogamy, mostly from heterosexual, married allies of the cause. But the site defines monogamy as being married to one person at a time, no matter how many sexual partners one has. When two gay men say they are monogamous, the vast majority of people assume they don't sleep around. From now on, I suggest, gays who say they are monogamous need to be asked if they mean monogamous using the usual connotation, or the little-known gay definition of having only one spouse.

The site quotes a therapist who criticizes sexual exclusivity as inadequate for male couples because of the nature of gay relationships.

Gay Couples Do Not Practice Monogamy

Also on the site is an article on marriage traditions, which claims that in Christianity, same-sex unions preceded male-female marriage; and that Western culture did not view monogamy as essential to marriage until the late Middle Ages. An essay on relationship tips gives 15 suggestions for working adultery into your marriage without going

Gay marriage opponents claim that the promiscuous gay lifestyle precludes a marital commitment.

© 2009 Keefe, The Denver Post, and PoliticalCartoons.com.

overboard. For example, it suggests, feel free to have extramarital sex in your home, but not in the bedroom.

Now, major gay organizations are scrupulous about not linking to sites that even link to gay pornography, for fear of being criticized. Yet it appears that for more than a decade, gay and lesbian groups have been recommending the Partners Task Force, and I have seen no evidence on the Web of any gay and lesbian people other than me objecting to that site's unusual definition of monogamy and its promotion of open marriages.

Nonmonogamous Relationships Are an Affront to the Institution of Marriage

If a straight organization such as the NAACP [National Association for the Advancement of Colored People], the Union for Reform Judaism, or the League of Women Voters linked to a Web site hostile to sexual fidelity that argued that adultery was consistent with monogamy, their members would be in an uproar because those ideas do not represent their values. But those ideas actually do represent mainstream gay and lesbian values, which is why there has been no uproar. The way to assess gay people's ideas is not through how they are portrayed in the mainstream media, where gays try to conform and be accepted. It is through the gay media, where they forget that anyone could be listening.

I find it strange that the *New York Times*, CNN, and other media pointed out the supposed contradiction in [Senator] David Vitter, R-La., opposing same-sex marriage while committing adultery, but I'm the only one who has complained that all four of the most prominent heterosexual politicians to have pushed for same-sex marriage (New York [governor] David Paterson and his predecessor Eliot Spitzer, as well as San Francisco Mayor Gavin Newsom and Los Angeles Mayor Antonio Villaraigosa) have admitted to adultery with one or more women. Think about it: Why wouldn't those guys want to extend marriage to people who think their philandering is compatible with the institution?

Gay Relationships Are Not Meant for Marriage

If you hear gay people objecting to the argument that same-sex marriage is fundamentally different from marriage, ask them if they consider sexual exclusivity (don't say monogamy because they might answer using the gay definition) an essential part of a proper marriage. Feel free to ask straight people the same question. Then you decide based on what you hear.

> **EVALUATING THE AUTHOR'S ARGUMENTS:**
>
> The author of this viewpoint, David Benkof, is a homosexual. Does it surprise you that a gay man would argue against the legalization of gay marriage? Why or why not? Explain your reasoning.

Legalized Gay Marriage Would Grant Rights to Gay People

Jan Vaughn Mock

"There are over 1,000 legal rights and benefits granted to federally recognized married couples that are denied to gay and lesbian couples who cannot get married."

When gay couples are not allowed to wed, they are denied the many rights that accompany heterosexual marriage, argues Jan Vaughn Mock in the following viewpoint. She discusses how, in an attempt to pacify gay activists, the state of California passed a law that granted gay couples rights as domestic partners. But Mock says that as mere domestic partners, gay couples are not entitled to more than one thousand rights afforded to legally married people. These include the right to be protected from divorce, the right to enjoy health and retirement benefits, the right to avoid special registration requirements, and more. Mock says that gay couples deserve to be granted the same rights that straight couples have and thus should be included in the institution of marriage.

Jan Vaughn Mock, "Domestic Partnership and Marriage: Separate and Unequal," *The Recorder,* December 5, 2008. Reproduced by permission.

Mock is a lawyer in San Francisco. Her articles have appeared in the *Recorder*, where this viewpoint was originally published.

AS YOU READ, CONSIDER THE FOLLOWING QUESTIONS:
1. What is the Domestic Partnership Act, according to the author? Why does she think it is insufficient?
2. In what way are gay couples not protected from divorce, according to the author?
3. What, in Mock's opinion, hampers a gay couple's ability to live and work wherever they wish in the country?

I n the wake of the passage of Proposition 8,[1] many have decried the importance of marriage to lesbian and gay Californians because, they claim, these couples already receive the same rights afforded by marriage under California's domestic partner laws. They are wrong.

Only Marriage Can Grant Rights

In response to the federal "Defense of Marriage Act," which denies to gay and lesbian couples the same rights and benefits afforded their heterosexual counterparts under federal law, the state of California enacted the Domestic Partnership Act. Because there are over 1,000 legal rights and benefits granted to federally recognized married couples that are denied to gay and lesbian couples who cannot get married, California tried to level the playing field.

The Domestic Partnership Act was intended to provide gay and lesbian couples with the same rights and benefits that heterosexual married couples enjoy under California law. Did California come close? Yes. But does domestic partnership equal marriage as the proponents of constitutional discrimination would have you believe? Decidedly not.

In order for domestic partnership to be the same as marriage under California law, several changes need to occur. Here are a few:

1. A 2008 California ballot initiative that overturned gay marriage in the state.

The Right to Avoid Registration and Cohabitation

In California, in order for a gay or lesbian couple to obtain the supposed "equivalent" of marriage under the Domestic Partnership Act, the couple must publicly register with the secretary of state. Married couples don't have to do that. Their identities can remain private. To achieve equality, married couples should be required to identify themselves on a public registry. (One can only imagine the outcry from unfaithful spouses!) Or alternatively, prospective domestic partners who want to keep their registration private should be able to do so.

Remember when your mother told you not to live with anyone before you got married? Gay and lesbian couples have no choice: California's domestic partnership law requires couples to live together before they can register. Not so for heterosexual couples. They can tie the knot after one romantic weekend in Napa [California]! Equality, then, mandates that all heterosexual couples must live together before a marriage license can be issued to them. Or conversely, that requirement should be eliminated from the domestic partner laws.

The Right to Marry Young and by Proxy

Young and in love? Too bad, if you're gay that is. While a young, straight couple under 18 can get married with either judicial or parental consent, gay and lesbian couples cannot. You must be 18 years old to register as domestic partners. Either young people should be allowed to make decisions for themselves without authoritarian approval or not. But the same rules should apply to everyone.

Is your loved one away, serving in the armed forces? If you want to be married by proxy (i.e., a 'stand in' bride or groom) you can. The marriage laws allow that. Again, not so for domestic partners. There is no such law that allows gay and lesbian couples to become domestic partners by proxy.

The Right to Be Protected from Divorce

Often (and curiously) touted by straight couples as a "benefit" of domestic partnership, no formal divorce is required should domestic partners choose to go their separate ways. Terminating a domestic partnership can be done simply by filing a one page form. Much of the cacophony [noise] around the "marriage" discussion has been about protecting the family unit, which of course includes protecting the financial welfare of spouses and children. As we all know either through personal experience or watching "Judge Judy," all divorces go through some minimum judicial review before the parties become legal strangers. This creates a significant deterrent to ending a marriage because of the complications and legal hoops that must be jumped through in order to get out of the relationship.

Gay couples argue that they are denied over one thousand legal rights that are granted to married heterosexual couples.

Gay and lesbian couples, on the other hand, have no such mandated protections (though there are limited exceptions). A domestic partner can be at risk in the event of a separation because, without judicial oversight, one partner can take off with an unfair portion of the community assets of the estate. One wonders how many married couples would give up their right to a judicially supervised divorce in order to achieve equality?

A married couple must live in California for at least six months before filing for divorce. Domestic partners have no such venue requirement. Equality dictates that either domestic partners have the same restrictions, or that married couples have no restrictions.

It is without serious dispute that these legal requirements were created as a deterrent against divorce. In order to achieve equality in trying to preserve the family unit, the same effort should be made to preserve and promote reconciliation between domestic partners as between straight married couples.

FAST FACT

According to Religious Tolerance.org, about eleven hundred rights are granted to legally married couples in the United States, such as employment benefits, life and health insurance rights, and inheritance rights.

The Right to Health and Retirement Benefits

Currently, heterosexual married couples can participate in their partner's health and retirement benefits provided under California's Long-Term Care Act. Not so for domestic partners. They are not entitled to any share of their partner's CalPERS [California Public Employees Retirement System] benefits, either while they are domestic partners, or thereafter. In order for domestic partnership and marriage to be equal, the state Family Code should be changed to allow domestic partners to receive these benefits just like married couples. And, of course, must we even discuss the inequity of giving veteran's benefits to a marital spouse but denying domestic partners those same benefits?

As a testament to the importance of marriage versus domestic partnership, married couples are required to solemnize their marriage. While this act of public commitment can be performed by clergy or a civil servant, it is the commitment itself that is mandated. "[T]he parties shall declare, in the physical presence of the person solemnizing the marriage and necessary witnesses, that they take each other as husband and wife." There is no such requirement for domestic partners. Thus, the face of the statutes themselves reveals the second-class status afforded to domestic partnerships and is faced with the legislative imprimatur [approval] that they are insignificant commitments.

In All Ways, Marriage Is Superior to Domestic Partnership

Why is marriage important to gay and lesbian couples? Easy. The above legal nuances aside, people marry because of love and commitment. Well, usually. We are, unfortunately, all too familiar with marriages for convenience. Nor can we ignore the Las Vegas-style weddings, which hardly promote the "sanctity of marriage," but which nonetheless are recognized as lawful, legal marriages and respected in every state. It matters not a wit that such farces might last no longer than a week.

"Marriage," not "domestic partnership," is a relationship recognized worldwide, in different cultures, countries and religions. There is a level of commitment embodied in a marriage that simply is not recognized by domestic partner laws. "Domestic partnerships" or "civil unions" are hard to explain. These couples have different levels of rights and responsibilities depending on which state they hail from. And their relationships may, or may not, be recognized in other states through which they travel or to which they might relocate.

Gay Couples Deserve the Same Rights as Straight Couples

After *Loving v. Virginia*, (1967) mandated the recognition of interracial marriage, every state in this country was required to recognize out-of-state marriages. Not so with civil unions and domestic partnerships, and certainly not true of gay and lesbian marriages, as we have seen from the rabid enactment of antigay legislation and initiatives across the nation. This hamstrings a gay and lesbian couple's ability to move freely throughout the country (a violation of the interstate commerce clause, perhaps?). They cannot take jobs in other states that do not recognize their relationship or family status, and they are not

A Wide Range of Rights

Because states allow or prohibit a variety of same-sex unions—ranging from domestic partnerships, to civil unions, to marriage—there is a range of diversity in the rights of same-sex couples. This map shows which states provide the most and fewest rights to same-sex partners.

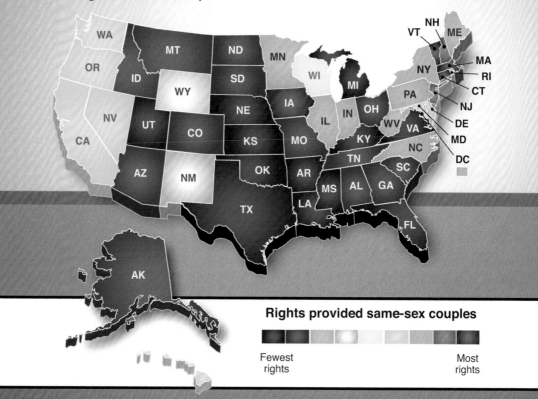

Taken from: *Los Angeles Times*, 2009.

afforded the protections of their straight, married counterparts when traveling around the country. Should married couples be required to remarry every time they go on a vacation, or move to another state for a job? Surely they should, if domestic partners are required to do so. But that will never happen. Until gay and lesbian couples are afforded the same legal protections as married couples, they remain faced with a host of legal rules and regulations and hoops to jump through to achieve equal status to marriage.

To continue to advance a position that domestic partnership is the same as marriage, and therefore gay and lesbian people should settle for domestic partnership, is simply insensate. This notion is not supported academically, legally, or dare I say spiritually. If marriage is the same thing as domestic partnership, then all couples in the state of California, straight or gay, should be satisfied to dub themselves domestic partners and to live by those standards. But proponents of inequality for California's gay and lesbian couples are unlikely to do that. Not now, and not ever. The inequality speaks for itself.

EVALUATING THE AUTHOR'S ARGUMENTS:

Jan Vaughn Mock argues that gay couples should be allowed to marry so they have access to the same rights that straight married couples enjoy. Do you think she is right? Is it fair to deny gay couples the rights that married straight couples enjoy? Or, do gay relationships not qualify for these rights? Explain your position using evidence from the texts you have read.

Viewpoint 6

Legalized Gay Marriage Would Threaten the Rights of Straight People

Thomas M. Messner

"*Redefining marriage to include same-sex unions poses significant threats to the religious liberties of people who continue to believe that marriage is a relationship between a man and a woman.*"

In the following viewpoint Thomas M. Messner argues that gay marriage threatens the rights of religious Americans. He explains that the majority of Americans are Christian, and as such, their religion prevents them from approving of or sanctioning homosexuality. But if gay marriage were to be legal, Messner says, religious Americans would be forced to accommodate gay relationships and events in ways that violate their religion. Messner concludes that changing the definition of marriage to accommodate gay couples is a direct violation of a person's right to practice his or her religion freely and openly, and as such cannot be sanctioned by the American government, which offers the freedom of religion to all citizens.

Messner is a visiting fellow at the Heritage Foundation, a conservative think tank that promotes public policy that favors free enterprise, limited government, and individual freedom.

AS YOU READ, CONSIDER THE FOLLOWING QUESTIONS:
1. In what way does Messner think legalized same-sex marriage could threaten religious institutions, churches, and public schools?
2. Why might faith-based charities be shut down if gay marriage becomes legal, according to Messner?
3. How does Messner say same-sex marriage would violate the rights of religious landlords and small-business owners?

Redefining marriage to include same-sex unions poses significant threats to the religious liberties of people who continue to believe that marriage is a relationship between a man and a woman. These threats have loomed large for several years, but recent developments, including the recent Connecticut and California judicial decisions redefining marriage to include same-sex unions, have refocused attention on the issue in a new, particularly urgent way.

A Threat to Religious Freedom

Our society has traditionally considered marriage to be an exclusive relationship between a man and a woman based on the understanding that marriage is a fundamental social institution ordered to the common good through the bearing and raising of children. But advocates of same-sex marriage consider the traditional understanding of marriage to be a form of irrational prejudice against homosexuals because it excludes them from marriage and the benefits that go with it. In this view, rationales regarding the bearing and raising of children are flawed or, at least, insufficient bases for defining marriage as a relationship between a man and a woman.

The idea that marriage is a relationship between a man and a woman is a core religious belief for significant numbers of Americans. But the freedom to express this and other beliefs about marriage, family, and sexual values will come under growing pressure as courts, public officials, and private institutions come to regard the traditional understanding of marriage as a form of irrational prejudice that should be purged from public life. The concept of marriage is too intertwined in our law and customs, and religious individuals and institutions are too integrated in the social and political lives of our communities, to avoid these conflicts.

Although this church-going man is pro-equality, some religious groups say that legalized gay marriage would threaten their core religious beliefs.

Specifically, in a society that redefines marriage to include same-sex unions, those who continue to believe marriage is a relationship between a man and a woman can expect to face three types of burdens.

A Burden on Churches, Schools, and Public Institutions

First, within the sphere of the administrative state, officials working out the implications of same-sex marriage will place several types of burdens on individuals and institutions that continue to believe marriage involves a man and a woman. For example, governments may require full acceptance of same-sex unions in programs or activities that are conducted or financially assisted by the state. Religious institutions that believe in marriage could lose equal access to public facilities. Churches that refuse to rent facilities for same-sex weddings could forfeit tax exemptions for those facilities. Public school students and teachers may be required to participate in classroom instruction about homosexual relationships that violates their religious beliefs. And public employees who express their belief in marriage could face the threat of discipline, demotion, and even termination.

Second, those who support the traditional understanding of marriage will be subject to even greater civil liability under nondiscrimination laws that prohibit private discrimination based on sexual orientation, marital status, and gender. Faith-based charities that provide valuable social services could be effectively shuttered by nondiscrimination laws that would require them to violate their religious beliefs by, for example, placing adopted children in same-sex households. Small-business owners could face significant liability under nondiscrimination laws that would force them to provide goods and services in situations—like same-sex weddings or civil union ceremonies—that violate their religious beliefs. Religious landlords, including religious educational institutions with married student housing, could encounter conflicts with their beliefs if forced to house same-sex couples under laws that prohibit discrimination based on marital status and sexual orientation. And professionals could be forced to violate their religious beliefs by nondiscrimination laws that, for example, would make it unlawful to decline to provide fertility services to a same-sex couple.

A Legal Nightmare Waiting to Happen

Although similar burdens can arise under nondiscrimination laws even in states that continue to define marriage as between one man and one woman, granting legal recognition to same-sex unions can reasonably be expected to amplify these burdens by significantly increasing the occasions of conflicts with religious liberty. In many cases, a person's sexual orientation is simply not relevant to the beliefs of individuals and institutions that support the traditional

Same-Sex Couples in the United States

Gay couples are heavily concentrated in just a few states. As a result, opponents of gay marriage say there is no reason to legalize it in most states.

Very high concentration
High concentration
Moderate concentration
Low concentration

Taken from: R. Bradley Sears et al. "Same-Sex Couples and Same-Sex Couples Raising Children in the United States," UCLA School of Law, September 2005.

understanding of marriage and therefore presents no conflict under nondiscrimination laws. But officially licensed same-sex unions involve a public recognition of sexual union, which means they can make orientation relevant and impossible to ignore where religious beliefs prohibit expressing support for or facilitating openly homosexual *conduct*. As a result, the number of potential religious liberty conflicts stemming from the application of nondiscrimination laws will increase significantly in states that grant legal recognition to same-sex unions.

Third, the existence of nondiscrimination laws, combined with the administrative policies of the state, can invite private forms of discrimination against religious individuals who believe that marriage involves a man and a woman and foster a climate of contempt for the public expression of their views. For example, private employers could become more likely to discipline or even terminate employees who express their beliefs about marriage or refuse to sign diversity statements requiring them to affirm same-sex unions. Religious professionals who consider same-sex unions to be immoral could also face serious conflicts if the *private* institutions that license and establish standards for social workers, counselors, attorneys, doctors, and members of other helping professions require applicants to condone same-sex relationships.

Gay Marriage Violates Americans' Right to Religious Freedom

America's long tradition of supporting religious freedom requires a full accounting of the dangers to religious liberty posed by redefining marriage. This tradition reflects the importance our society attaches to each person's duty to honor his or her conscience and the role religious freedom plays in securing the rights of all citizens to be free from undue coercion by the state. Because religious freedom is a precondition for a civil and free society, citizens of all faiths—and no faith at all—have a deep interest in protecting the rights of others to honor the dictates of their conscience even when others, or even a majority of others, would reach a different conclusion.

Preserving marriage as a relationship between a man and a woman is the most effective way to avoid the dangers to religious liberty associated with granting legal recognition to same-sex unions. At a minimum, however, lawmakers should provide exemptions where changes in marriage policies and nondiscrimination laws would force individuals and institutions to violate their beliefs.

EVALUATING THE AUTHOR'S ARGUMENTS:

Thomas M. Messner views gay marriage as a threat to the rights of nongay Americans. But supporters of same-sex marriage say it is the rights of gay people that suffer when same-sex marriage is prohibited. What do you think? The rights of which group of Americans are most violated by either the legalization of or prohibition of gay marriage? Why?

Chapter 3

Does Gay Marriage Threaten Society?

The open rancor of people on both sides of the gay marriage debate often obscures the issue itself.

Gay Marriage Threatens Society

"We know it's best for children and for society that men and women get married. We know it's healthier. We know it's better for men. We know it's better for women. We know it's better for communities."

Rick Santorum, interviewed by David Masci

Legalized gay marriage would pose a threat to American society, argues Rick Santorum in the following viewpoint. He thinks this in part because gay marriage is an untested and unproven social experiment. He says gay rights activists have no studies proving that gay marriage would help the country and no data to show that their unions would improve America's morality or help its children. The only thing gay rights advocates have done, in Santorum's opinion, is make the case that they want to get married. But Santorum says this is not enough of a reason to fundamentally change the definition of marriage, an institution that is incredibly valuable to the functioning of America. He concludes that gay marriages violate the Judeo-Christian principles upon which America was founded and for this reason should be seen as a threat to society.

Santorum served in Congress as a senator from Pennsylvania from 1994 to 2006. He is now a senior fellow with the Ethics and Public Policy Center.

Masci is a senior researcher at the Pew Forum on Religion & Public Life.

David Masci, "An Argument Against Same-Sex Marriage: An Interview with Rick Santorum," Pew Forum on Religion & Public Life, www.pewforum.org, April 24, 2008. Reproduced by permission.

AS YOU READ, CONSIDER THE FOLLOWING QUESTIONS:
  1. What are environmental impact studies, and how does Santorum factor them into his argument?
  2. What does Santorum say happened in the Netherlands once gay marriage was legalized?
  3. Why, in Santorum's opinion, are Americans afraid to speak out against gay marriage?

D avid Masci: *Gay rights advocates and others say that gay and lesbian people want to get married for the same reasons that straight people do—they want to be in caring, stable relationships, they want to build a life and even start a family with someone else. Why shouldn't they be able to do this?*

Gays Have Not Proven Why Their Marriages Would Help Society

Rick Santorum: See, I think that's the foundational flaw with this whole debate. The law is as it has been for 200-plus years, and so the burden is on them to make the persuasive case as to why they should be married, not just for their benefit but for what the impact is on society and marriage as a whole, and on children.

I would argue that the gay community has not made the argument. They may have made the argument as to why they want it, but they have not made any arguments as to why this is beneficial for society. They have not made any argument—convincing or otherwise, that I'm aware of—as to what the impact would be on heterosexual marriages and what the impact would be on children.

They have no studies. They have no information whatsoever about what it would do to the moral ecology of the country, what it would do to religious liberty, what it would do to the mental and physical health of children—nothing. They've made no case. Basically the case they've made is, "We want what you want, and therefore you should give it to us."

So you're saying that advocates of same-sex marriage are not seeing the big picture?

Yes. I have a book that was written a few years ago called *It Takes a Family*. In that book I have a chapter on moral ecology, and I explain that if you go to the National Archives, you will come to a section that has, as far as the eye can see, rows and rows and rows of environmental impact statements, because we have laws in this country that say before you go out and you put in a bridge across a creek, you have to go out and see whether what you're doing is disturbing the landscape there.

Yet when it comes to something that I happen to believe is actually more important than a particular plot of land—the entire moral ecology of our country, who we are as a people, what we stand for, what we teach our children, what our values and ethics are—people argue that we can build the equivalent of a strip mall without even thinking about what those consequences are. . . .

Former Pennsylvania senator Rick Santorum (pictured) believes that legalizing gay marriage would unravel the moral fabric of American society.

American Law Must Encourage What Is Best for Society

Another argument made by gay rights advocates is that with or without marriage, gay families are already a widespread reality. They point out that we already have gay couples living together, some with children. And they ask: Isn't it better that they be legally married to each other, if for no other reason than for the benefit and the welfare of the children?

The answer is no—because of the consequences to society as a whole. And again, those are consequences that they choose to ignore. What society should be about is encouraging what's best for children. What's best for children, we know, is a mother and a father who are the parents of that child, raising that child in a stable, married relationship, and we should have laws that encourage that, that support that.

What you're talking about with same-sex marriage is completely deconstructing marriage and taking away a privilege that is given to two people, a man and a woman who are married, who have a child or adopt a child. We know it's best for children and for society that men and women get married. We know it's healthier. We know it's better for men. We know it's better for women. We know it's better for communities.

What we don't know is what happens with other options. And once you get away from the model of "what we know is best" and you get into the other options, from my perspective, there's no stopping it. And also from my perspective, you devalue what you want to value, which is a man and woman in marriage with a child or children. And when you devalue that, you get less of it. When you get less of it, society as a whole suffers.

If Marriage Becomes Meaningless, All of Society Will Suffer

Do you feel confident that if same-sex marriage became the norm in our society that we would get less traditional marriage?

The answer is yes, because marriage then becomes, to some degree, meaningless. I mean, if anybody can get married for any reason, then it loses its special place. And, you know, it's already lost its special place, in many respects, because of divorce. The institution of marriage is already under assault. So why should we do more to discredit it and harm it?

Stanley Kurtz of the Ethics and Public Policy Center has written extensively about this, about what the impact is in countries that have adopted same-sex marriage. We have, in fact, seen a decline in the number of marriages, a delay in people getting married, more children being born out of wedlock and higher rates of divorce. None of those things are good for society. None of those things are good for children.

But can you lay these changes at the feet of same-sex marriage?

Yes, I think you can lay them at its feet. Kurtz notes that the marriage rate in the Netherlands was always actually one of the lowest in the EU [European Union]. And once same-sex marriage was put in place, it broke below the line.

Dangerously Close to Losing Our Values

As a person who has positioned himself as a defender of Christian values, why is gay marriage particularly opposed to those values?

Well, the laws in this country are built upon a certain worldview, and it is the Judeo-Christian worldview. And that worldview has been expressed in our laws on marriage for 200-plus years. Up until 25 years ago, we would never have sat here and done this interview. It would have been beyond the pale. And so it is clearly a dramatic departure from the Judeo-Christian ethic that is reflected in our laws that say marriage is a sacred union between a man and a woman.

When you look ahead, do you feel optimistic that your side in this debate will ultimately prevail?

What I've noticed about this debate is that fewer and fewer people are stepping up and taking the position I'm taking because they see the consequences of doing so. I don't think there is an issue that is a tougher issue for people to stand up against in American culture today than this one, both from the standpoint of the mainstream media and the popular culture condemning you for your—they can

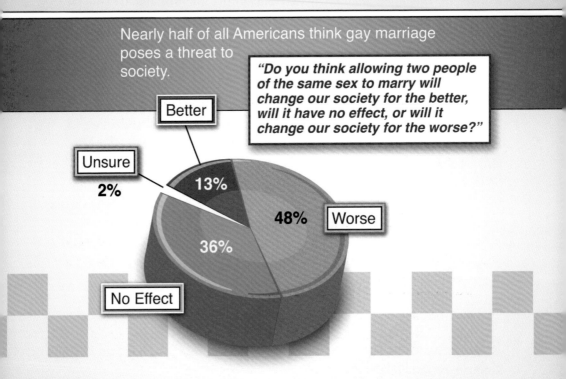

Americans Fear Gay Marriage

Nearly half of all Americans think gay marriage poses a threat to society.

"Do you think allowing two people of the same sex to marry will change our society for the better, will it have no effect, or will it change our society for the worse?"

Better 13%

Unsure 2%

Worse 48%

No Effect 36%

Taken from: *USA Today*/Gallup Poll, May 7–10, 2009.

use all sorts of words to describe you—intolerant, bigot, homophobe, hater. The other side takes it personally. And so it makes it very difficult for folks to stand up and argue public policy when the other side views it as a personal, direct assault on them. So it's very, very hard for me to be optimistic when we have a battle of ideas and one side is universally hammered for being intolerant bigots and the other side is enlightened and tolerant—which I think is false, but it is the pervasive attitude.

Americans Don't Want Same-Sex Marriage

We know that the American public doesn't approve of same-sex marriage, but they are uncomfortable about it because, again, the public perception is if you feel that way, you're a bigot or a hater. And if the culture continues to send that message, if our educational system sends that message, which it does, you know, eventually the culture will change and people's opinions will change.

The push back is what most people know: that mothers and fathers bring something unique. I mean, I have six children. I know that two mothers would not be able to give to my children what a mother and a father can give to my children. For instance, my daughter's relationship with men is, in many respects, formed by her relationship with me. There are volumes of evidence showing that if little girls don't have a father, it impacts their ability as adults to bond with men in healthy relationships.

What do we know, really, about children raised by same-sex couples? We're into, in many respects, an unknown territory. There is already a difficult environment for children in America today, at least from the traditional Judeo-Christian perspective. So I think this is a fight worth fighting, even if it's not a popular fight.

EVALUATING THE AUTHOR'S ARGUMENTS:

To make his argument, Rick Santorum questions the morality of gay unions and says they conflict with Judeo-Christian principles. What does he mean by this? Do you agree? Why or why not? Ground your reasoning in your own personal beliefs.

Gay Marriage Strengthens Society

Jonathan Rauch

"*America needs more marriages, not fewer, and the best way to encourage marriage is to encourage marriage, which is what society does by bringing gay couples inside the tent.*"

In the following viewpoint Jonathan Rauch explains why legalizing gay marriage would benefit everyone in America. When gay couples are not allowed to marry, they are doomed to a world of instability, loneliness, and lawlessness. Their relationships are less committed and more adulterous than married relationships, and Rauch says commitment and fidelity help build strong families and thus strong communities. Moreover, married people are more likely to be healthier, happier, and wealthier, and children raised in married environments are also likely to be protected against financial, medical, and emotional instability. All of these components are the fabric of a strong America. For this reason, Rauch believes that all Americans can benefit from legalizing gay marriage.

Rauch is a senior writer with the *National Journal* and the author of *Gay Marriage: Why It Is Good for Gays, Good for Straights, and Good for America.*

AS YOU READ, CONSIDER THE FOLLOWING QUESTIONS:
1. What, according to Rauch, is the monument of marriage-deprived gay society? What does he mean by this?
2. What do two partners and their community agree on through marriage, according to Rauch?
3. What does Rauch say are the two ways to see the legal marriage of Del Martin and Phyllis Lyon?

By order of its state Supreme Court, California began legally marrying same-sex couples this week.[1] The first to be wed in San Francisco were Del Martin and Phyllis Lyon, pioneering gay-rights activists who have been a couple for more than 50 years.

More ceremonies will follow, at least until November, when gay marriage will go before California's voters. They should choose to keep it. To understand why, imagine your life without marriage. Meaning, not merely your life if you didn't happen to get married. What I am asking you to imagine is life without even the possibility of marriage.

Life Without the Possibility of Marriage

Re-enter your childhood, but imagine your first crush, first kiss, first date and first sexual encounter, all bereft of any hope of marriage as a destination for your feelings. Re-enter your first serious relationship, but think about it knowing that marrying the person is out of the question.

Imagine that in the law's eyes you and your soul mate will never be more than acquaintances. And now add even more strangeness. Imagine coming of age into a whole community, a whole culture, without marriage and the bonds of mutuality and kinship that go with it.

What is this weird world like? It has more sex and less commitment than a world with marriage. It is a world of fragile families living on the shadowy outskirts of the law; a world marked by heightened fear of loneliness or abandonment in crisis or old age; a world in some

---

1. These marriages were invalidated when California voters elected to prohibit gay marriage in November 2008.

respects not even civilized, because marriage is the foundation of civilization.

This was the world I grew up in. The AIDS quilt is its monument.

Few heterosexuals can imagine living in such an upside-down world, where love separates you from marriage instead of connecting you with it. Many don't bother to try. Instead, they say same-sex couples can get the equivalent of a marriage by going to a lawyer and drawing up paperwork—as if heterosexual couples would settle for anything of the sort.

Even a moment's reflection shows the fatuousness [foolishness] of "Let them eat contracts." No private transaction excuses you from testifying in court against your partner, or entitles you to Social Security survivor benefits, or authorizes joint tax filing, or secures U.S. residency for your partner if he or she is a foreigner. I could go on and on.

Marriage Binds Communities

Marriage, remember, is not just a contract between two people. It is a contract that two people make, as a couple, with their community—which is why there is always a witness. Two people can't go into a room by themselves and come out legally married. The partners agree to take care of each other so the community doesn't have to. In exchange, the community deems them a family, binding them to each other and to society with a host of legal and social ties.

This is a fantastically fruitful bargain. Marriage makes you, on average, healthier, happier and wealthier. If you are a couple raising kids, marrying is likely to make them healthier, happier and wealthier, too. Marriage is our first and best line of defense against financial, medical and emotional meltdown. It provides domesticity and a safe harbor for sex. It stabilizes communities by formalizing responsibilities and creating kin networks. And its absence can be calamitous, whether in inner cities or gay ghettos.

Society Needs Gay Marriage

In 2008, denying gay Americans the opportunity to marry is not only inhumane, it is unsustainable. History has turned a corner: Gay couples—including gay parents—live openly and for the most part comfortably in mainstream life. This will not change, ever.

Gay marriage proponents believe that gay couples have much to offer their communities.

Because parents want happy children, communities want responsible neighbors, employers want productive workers, and governments want smaller welfare caseloads, society has a powerful interest in recognizing and supporting same-sex couples. It will either fold them into marriage or create alternatives to marriage, such as publicly recognized and subsidized cohabitation. Conservatives often say same-sex marriage should be prohibited because it does not exemplify the ideal form of family. They should consider how much less ideal an example gay couples will set by building families and raising children out of wedlock.

Gay Marriage Will Not Lead to Social Ills

Nowadays, even opponents of same-sex marriage generally concede it would be good for gay people. What they worry about are the possible secondary effects it could have as it ramifies through law and society. What if gay marriage becomes a vehicle for polygamists who want to marry multiple partners, egalitarians who want to radically rewrite family law, or secularists who want to suppress religious objections to homosexuality?

> **FAST FACT**
>
> Five years after legalizing gay marriage, Massachusetts had the lowest divorce rate in the United States, according to data from the National Center for Vital Statistics. In 2008 its divorce rates were on par with what the nation's had been in 1940.

Space doesn't permit me to treat those and other objections in detail, beyond noting that same-sex marriage no more leads logically to polygamy than giving women one vote leads to giving men two; that gay marriage requires only few and modest changes to existing family law; and that the Constitution provides robust protections for religious freedom.

I'll also note, in passing, that these arguments conscript homosexuals into marriagelessness in order to stop heterosexuals from making bad decisions, a deal to which we gay folks say, "Thanks, but no thanks." We wonder how many heterosexuals would give up their own marriage, or for that matter their own divorce, to discourage other people from making poor policy choices. Any volunteers?

Allowing Same-Sex Marriage Helps Everyone

Honest advocacy requires acknowledging that same-sex marriage *is* a significant social change and, as such, is not risk-free. I believe the risks are modest, manageable, and likely to be outweighed by the benefits. Still, it's wise to guard against unintended consequences by trying gay marriage in one or two states and seeing what happens, which is exactly what the country is doing.

By the same token, however, honest opposition requires acknowledging that there are risks and unforeseen consequences on both sides of the equation. Some of the unforeseen consequences of allowing same-sex marriage will be good, not bad. And barring gay marriage is risky in its own right.

America needs more marriages, not fewer, and the best way to encourage marriage is to encourage marriage, which is what society does by bringing gay couples inside the tent. A good way to discourage marriage, on the other hand, is to tarnish it as discriminatory in the minds of millions of young Americans. Conservatives who object to redefining marriage risk redefining it themselves, as a civil-rights violation.

There are two ways to see the legal marriage of Del Martin and Phyllis Lyon. One is as the start of something radical: an experiment that jeopardizes millennia of accumulated social patrimony. The other is as the *end* of something radical: an experiment in which gay people were told that they could have all the sex and love they could find, but they could not even think about marriage. If I take the second view, it is on conservative—in fact, traditional—grounds that gay souls and straight society are healthiest when sex, love and marriage all walk in step.

EVALUATING THE AUTHORS' ARGUMENTS:

At the core of Jonathan Rauch's argument is the suggestion that strong families—whether gay or straight—make for a strong America. How do you think Rick Santorum, interviewed in the previous viewpoint, would respond to this claim? After explaining Santorum's perspective, state your own. Do you ultimately agree with Rauch or Santorum?

Gay Marriage Threatens Children

Margret Kopala

"We need fewer, not more, orphans and that means a family bus that is driven by mothers and fathers."

In the following viewpoint Margret Kopala explains why she believes that legalizing gay marriage threatens children. Children do best when they are raised by both fathers and mothers, she says. It is in such an environment that boys learn how to be husbands and girls learn how to be wives. But when children are raised by "parents" rather than fathers and mothers, they are at a social disadvantage and are more likely to have behavioral problems and difficulty sustaining relationships. Kopala concludes that today's children are already threatened by high rates of divorce, single parenthood, and orphanhood—legalizing gay marriage will only encourage the disintegration of the traditional family that children need to thrive.

Kopala is the director of research and policy development at the Canadian Centre for Policy Studies.

Margret Kopala, "Sacrificing Our Children for Same-Sex 'Marriage,'" World Net Daily, May 21, 2008. Reproduced by permission.

AS YOU READ, CONSIDER THE FOLLOWING QUESTIONS:
1. What does Kopala mean when she says that few people would let a blind person drive a bus?
2. What does Kopala say the consequences are for changing the words "husband" and "father" to "spouse" and "parent"?
3. According to Kopala, what is the wrong way to address intolerance and discrimination toward homosexuals?

Explaining its recent [2008] decision to legalize same-sex "marriage," the Supreme Court of California rightly refrained from offering any judgment about it as policy; rather, the court limited its consideration to the constitutional validity of same-sex "marriage." But like Canadian same-sex "marriage" advocates, it erred when it compared the ban on same-sex "marriage" with the ban on interracial marriage that was overturned in 1948 [in California].

Fundamentally Changing Marriage

The issue is not who is allowed on the "bus," but rather, who is driving the bus. Few would allow the blind or otherwise incapacitated to do this job. Though marriage performs many functions, it is also society's premier institution for conceiving and nurturing children, and this involves gender specific roles. The bus being the family, the question becomes who should be its designated driver?

The argument placed by counsel for the Government of Alberta before Canada's Supreme Court in 2004 on this issue is even more to the point. Any change to the opposite sex requirement of marriage is a change to the nature of marriage itself, he said. Equality guarantees are not a vehicle for remaking fundamental social institutions in an effort to manage questions of social status and approval. Only by elevating incapacity to inequality does the gay marriage movement make any sense, he added.

In other words, interracial marriage doesn't change the institution. Same-sex "marriage" does. . . .

Orphaning Our Youth

Not long ago, Lord William Rees-Mogg lamented in *The Times* how British liberties were being orphaned in the controversy over the

Catholic Church's refusal to arrange adoptions for same-sex couples. As [writer] Jacques Barzun observes in *From Dawn to Decadence,* while the traditional family has not disappeared, the variants are becoming traditional themselves: children lacking one or another biological parent exist in single-parent families, blended families, families rearing grandchildren and homosexual couples with a child, adopted or not. "Out of these situations arose two novelties," he writes, "the day care center and the semi-orphan."

Orphan is a word that has also appeared in Canada where the Charter of Rights and Freedoms sanctions religious freedoms and, according to a Supreme Court reference in 2004, same-sex "marriage." Opposition to same-sex "marriage" in Canada nonetheless continues. While most support the right of homosexuals to seek and to have their unions ratified in law (civil unions were never an accepted option for Canada's same-sex "marriage" activists), opposition is more generally coalescing around the right of children to be raised, as nearly as possible, by their biological parents.

> ## FAST FACT
>
> According to the UCLA Williams Project on Sexual Orientation Law and Public Policy, the median household income for same-sex parents in the United States is $10,000 lower than for different-sex parents. In addition, the home ownership rate for same-sex parents is 15 percent lower than that for different-sex parents.

Children Need Fathers and Mothers

Canada's leading spokesperson on this issue is Margaret Somerville. Somerville, a bio-ethicist and Samuel Gale Chair in Law, is also a professor in the faculty of medicine at McGill University in Montreal. She reminds us that, under international law, marriage confers the right to found a family. In Canada, this means same-sex couples can adopt children as well as access reproductive technologies for this purpose even though a growing body of evidence reveals that the adult children of any arrangement that departs from traditional family norms are disadvantaged, including the children of divorce and donor conceived children. Notably, a meta-study undertaken by

Swedish scientists and published in the March 2008 edition of *Acta Paediatrica,* confirms that children need fathers as well as mothers.

The key here is the *adult* children of such arrangements. While most studies focus on the seemingly benign or at least manageable effects of non-traditional arrangements on children and adolescents, longitudinal studies reveal a different picture of what happens when they mature. At the University of California in Berkeley, for instance, psychologist Judith Wallerstein demonstrated in a 30-year longitudinal study how the first group have difficulty as mature adults finding suitable partners and then sustaining their relationships. Writing in *The Legacy of Divorce*, she explains that they lack the role models most effectively secured by a child's married biological parents.

Likewise, Margaret Somerville's numerous articles discuss how members of the second group (who refer to themselves as "genetic"

Same-Sex Parents Have Fewer Economic Resources than Married Parents

Comparisons of households with same-sex couples raising children and married couples raising children reveal that same-sex parents have fewer economic resources to provide for their children. Opponents of gay marriage say this shows one of the ways that gay marriage would put children at a disadvantage.

Household characteristics	Same-sex couples	Married couples
B.A. or advanced degree	23%	30%
Percent homeowners	64%	78%
Household income (average)	$65,501	$76,403
Household income (median)	$51,900	$60,700
Median property values	$112,500	$137,500

Taken from: R. Bradley Sears et al. "Same-sex Couples and Same-Sex Couples Raising Children in the United States," UCLA School of Law, September 2005.

orphans), experience intense feelings of abandonment by the donor parent. Meanwhile, Kay Hymowitz's *Marriage and Caste in America* demonstrates the role played by fragmenting family structures in rising inequalities. This on top of evidence that young men who grow up without fathers seek to have their approval and authority needs met by joining gangs.

How adoptive same-sex couples might navigate this minefield is anybody's guess given that opposite-sex couples have themselves performed so miserably.

Dangerously Changing What Words Mean

In any case, equating homosexual and heterosexual relationships is challenging enough, though in Canada, activist judges and legislators are deploying all of their creative talent to find a way. Gays and lesbians, for instance, cannot be husbands and wives or mothers and fathers, at least not in relationships with each other. The Canadian solution? Change the language. Legislation at both provincial and federal levels has been amended to remove the words "husband" and "wife." In Canada, we are all "spouses" now. Meanwhile, the Civil Marriage Act that institutionalized same-sex "marriage" in 2005 also eliminated any reference to "natural" parents in federal law, substituting the term "legal" parent. More recently, the Ontario Court of Appeal ruled in a case where a child of a sperm donor that is being raised by its mother and her lesbian "spouse" that children can have more than two "parents." Now, any number of "parents" will effectively be allowed on a child's birth certificate.

The consequences of such changes seem not to have occurred to anyone. What, for instance, does the son of two lesbian mothers learn about what it means to be a husband? What does he learn from a two-day a week dad, or one he will never meet, about what it means to be a father? And that's before issues concerning precedents for legalizing polygamy and other polyamorous relationships arise. . . .

We Should Seek the Best for Our Children

For Californians, the danger exists in deferring to a celebrity and intellectual class that has decreed that same-sex "marriage," as well as a host of other family arrangements, is acceptable. Yet by habitually defaulting to the minimally acceptable option in an attempt to accommodate all, we virtually guarantee the minimum not the optimal for our children.

It is understandable that as a society we should want to address intolerance and discrimination directed toward homosexuals, but it is a profound mistake to attempt to do this by passing laws that

Anti–gay marriage activists assert that because children are raised by gay "parents," rather than by mothers and fathers, they are more likely to be socially disadvantaged.

fundamentally alter existing social norms and institutions. Whatever the anthropology, social science demonstrates clearly that the needs of children coincide with the received wisdom of the ages articulated in our customs, traditions and, yes, our religions.

We need fewer, not more, orphans and that means a family bus that is driven by mothers and fathers.

EVALUATING THE AUTHOR'S ARGUMENTS:

Margret Kopala considers children who are not raised by their biological mothers and fathers to be in a state of orphanhood. Do you agree with this characterization? Why or why not? Explain your reasoning, and then say whether you agree with her position that gay marriage is bad for children.

Gay Marriage Nurtures Children

Sara Miles

"Lesbians and gays are not going to stop having kids because we can't marry. Our children are not going to disappear."

Allowing gay couples to marry is in the best interest of children, argues Sara Miles in the following viewpoint. She offers up her own family as evidence of why gay parents make great parents and why prohibiting gay couples from marrying only hurts children. She says she and her wife love their daughter Katie as much as any straight couple, but Katie is banned from reaping the benefits that a straight couple's kid would get from her parents. Katie is not allowed to get health insurance through her other mother, and their family cannot benefit from the tax breaks that are afforded straight families. Miles argues that gay people are always going to have children, but forcing them to do so out of marriage is harmful. Legalizing gay marriage lets gays raise children in the safest, most secure, and financially stable environment possible, which Miles says is ultimately in every child's best interest.

Miles is the author of the book *Take This Bread: A Radical Conversion.*

Sara Miles, "Ban on Gay Marriage Denies Justice to Children," Salon.com, July 10, 2006. This article first appeared in Salon.com, at www.salon.com. An online version remains in the Salon archives. Reprinted with permission.

AS YOU READ, CONSIDER THE FOLLOWING QUESTIONS:
1. By 2000, what percent of American households does Miles say consisted of a married straight couple with children?
2. What percent of the births of straight people occur out of wedlock, according to Miles?
3. In the author's opinion, what will the courts eventually catch up to?

There's nothing like a judicial ruling—in this case, the extremely tortured one written last week [in July 2006] by Judge Robert S. Smith of the New York Court of Appeals against gay marriage—to make me feel simultaneously all-powerful and helpless. On Friday, my family read the news over breakfast. I was on my way to volunteer at my church food pantry; my wife was finishing the endless paperwork for our 17-year-old daughter's college loan, and Katie—one of the "children" in whose interest the court said it ruled—was on her way out the door to her summer job.

Who knew we could have such a grandiose impact? Just by hanging out in our kitchen, the three of us challenge what Smith called the "accepted truth for almost everyone who ever lived, in any society in which marriage existed, that there could be marriages only between participants of different sex." By asking for the legal benefits of marriage, we threaten the already unstable institution of the heterosexual family.

It Is Wrong to Assume Gay Marriage Hurts Children

Judge Smith's decision posited two major reasons to "rationally support" the ban on gay marriage—both of them grounded in the assumption, which I share, that marriage is important to the welfare of children. After a few factually incorrect preambles (note to judge: Not all gay couples become parents through adoption or "technological marvels"; we can tell you how reproduction works later, in private) he launched his argument.

First, the judge delivered a surprising attack on the heterosexual agenda: Straight people, he said, are really bad at marriage. Opposite-sex relationships, wrote the judge, are often "casual" or temporary.

(Wasn't that what right-wing frothers used to say about queers?) Thus, wayward, irresponsible, sexually promiscuous straight people need the legal benefits of marriage as inducements (read: special prizes nobody else gets) to lure them into "solemn, long-term commitments" to each other, so that they can care responsibly for children. Were we to extend those privileges to homosexuals . . . well, they wouldn't be privileges anymore, would they?

Second, the judge declared, it's best for children to grow up with a mother and a father. Though he admitted there is no scientific evidence to support this assertion, "common sense," he said, makes it so. (If we're going to be commonsensical, your honor, the children of lesbian and gay families also have "living models of what both a man and a woman are like"—surprisingly, few of us raise our kids in single-sex dormitories surrounded by barbed wire. And if the point is a variety of role models, why allow single straight people to adopt?)

Straight Couples Have Threatened Marriage and Children

It's understandable that the judge would be worried about the institution of marriage. Straight people are just not that into marriage anymore. By 2000, only 25 percent of American households consisted of a married heterosexual couple with children. Legal marriage gives heterosexuals the right to hire a cheesy '70s cover band, read embarrassing poetry to their friends, and fight with their parents over whom to invite to a party with bad food. (It also allows couples to go broke together: Marriage is an $85 billion a year industry.) And marriage is hard to sustain: For heterosexual couples, who can divorce the min-

FAST FACT

The American Bar Association estimates that 4 million gay and lesbian parents are raising 8 to 10 million children in the United States.

ute they're tired of their sacred vows, about half of all marriages end in divorce. Legal marriage carries many responsibilities: among them the duty of parents, unmet by 62 percent of divorced fathers, to support their children. Increasing numbers of straight people don't bother: Over a third of all births are out of wedlock.

Judge Smith recognized these difficulties, arguing with syntactical wobbliness but undeniable fervor that the institution of heterosexual marriage needs propping up. He even suggested, counterintuitively, that "unstable relationships between people of the opposite sex present a greater danger that children will be born into or grow up in unstable homes than is the case with same-sex couples."

Gay Parents Make Great Parents

But the judge's solution—keep queers out of the mix—doesn't work, if he really wants marriage to be about the welfare of children. First of all, as Judge Judith Kaye wrote in her dissenting opinion, "while encouraging opposite-sex couples to marry before they have children is certainly a legitimate interest of the state, the exclusion of gay men and lesbians from marriage in no way furthers this interest. There are enough marriage licenses to go around for everyone."

Furthermore, if the courts should encourage marriages that help kids, why aren't the courts supporting the more-likely-to-be-stable relationships of gay couples?

And finally, what do the courts have to say about the rights of the kids in lesbian and gay families? Or, to get personal about it, what about the rights of my brilliant, beautiful, adored daughter, with her two mothers and gay father? Katie's father and I, her biological parents, were never married; her mothers were married, briefly, in the great civic uprising of February 2004 in San Francisco. (That marriage was quickly annulled by the courts, making us ex-wives living together raising a child, a category not frequently found in surveys of marriage statistics.)

All of Katie's parents have supported her, caring for her in sickness and laughing ourselves silly over her jokes; all of us have argued with her about cleaning up her room; all of us are preparing for tears and pride as she heads off to college this fall. Our daughter, like all children, deserves what Judge Smith recognized as "an important function of marriage"—to "create more stability and permanence in the relationships that cause children to be born." She also deserves the legal benefits and protections afforded to the kids of heterosexual parents—even unmarried heterosexual parents. (In 1968, the Supreme Court swept away many of the harsher provisions of common law

Millions of American Children Have at Least One Gay Parent

Though no one knows exactly how many children are being raised in gay households, millions of Americans have at least one gay parent. Supporters of gay marriage say these children will benefit if their parents are allowed to marry.

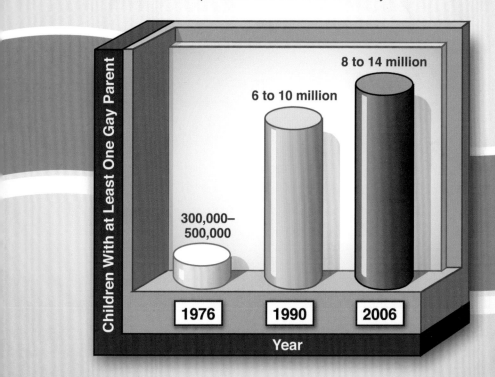

Taken from: Child Welfare Information Gateway and the Partners Task Force.

governing illegitimacy, ruling on equal protection grounds.) She deserves to have Martha recognized as her mother.

Banning Gay Marriage Denies Rights to Kids

And this is where I feel powerless.

It's bad enough that the state treats me and my wife and Katie's father as unworthy to share in full citizenship. But it's unforgivable that our child, too, is penalized for our inability to marry. She

The author contends that banning same-sex marriage ultimately harms children by denying them rights available to children of straight couples.

can't claim Martha as a family member; she can't get insurance coverage through Martha or be treated as Martha's child for tax, probate or healthcare matters; she has no legal relationship with the woman who's helped raise her since she was in kindergarten and a boy made her cry. "You don't even exist," that boy told Katie, with Judge Smith's impeccable logic. "You have to be married to have a baby, and your parents aren't married, so you weren't even born, ha ha."

The fact is, lesbians and gays are not going to stop having kids because we can't marry. Our children are not going to disappear.

Which brings me back to feeling powerful—seriously. As we've seen in South Africa and Eastern Europe and San Francisco, civil society in its richness is always greater than official codes about who is, and isn't, a full person. Katie and a million kids like her are here, and their families will continue to thrive. At some point, the courts will catch up.

EVALUATING THE AUTHOR'S ARGUMENTS:

In addition to using facts and examples to make her argument, Sara Miles uses the story of her daughter Katie to show how banning gay marriage hurts the children of gay people. Did reading this story influence your opinion of her argument? Did it personalize this issue for you and make you any more likely to agree with her? Why or why not?

Gay Marriage Would Lead to Polygamy

Charles Krauthammer

"It is utterly logical for polygamy rights to follow gay rights."

Charles Krauthammer is a nationally syndicated conservative columnist. In the following viewpoint he argues that legalizing gay marriage would naturally lead to polygamy, or marriages among groups of people. He explains that marriage currently consists of two people of opposite genders. But gay marriage supporters want to change half of that equation. In Krauthammer's opinion, once you change half of that equation, there is nothing to stop the other half from being altered. Furthermore, Krauthammer says that polygamy is gaining acceptance as an alternative lifestyle. In fact, it has an even stronger historical basis than gay marriage does. For this reason, Krauthammer predicts that polygamists will soon be the next group claiming to want equal rights under the institution, and it will be hard to deny them that once the definition of marriage is so fundamentally changed.

Charles Krauthammer, "Pandora and Polygamy," *Washington Post,* March 17, 2007. Reproduced by permission of the author.

AS YOU READ, CONSIDER THE FOLLOWING QUESTIONS:

1. How does the HBO series *Big Love* factor into the author's argument?
2. What problem does Krauthammer see resulting from gay activists' fight against higher and lower orders of love?
3. When and where in history has polygamy been an accepted behavior, according to Krauthammer?

And now, polygamy.

With the sweetly titled HBO series *Big Love*, polygamy comes out of the closet. Under the headline "Polygamists, Unite!" *Newsweek* informs us of "polygamy activists emerging in the wake of the gay-marriage movement." Says one evangelical Christian big lover: "Polygamy rights is the next civil-rights battle."

Changing Marriage Opens It to Gays and Polygamists

Polygamy used to be stereotyped as the province of secretive Mormons, primitive Africans and profligate Arabs. With *Big Love* it moves to suburbia as a mere alternative lifestyle.

As *Newsweek* notes, these stirrings for the mainstreaming of polygamy (or, more accurately, polyamory[1]) have their roots in the increasing legitimization of gay marriage. In an essay 10 years ago, I pointed out that it is utterly logical for polygamy rights to follow gay rights. After all, if traditional marriage is defined as the union of (1) two people of (2) opposite gender, and if, as advocates of gay marriage insist, the gender requirement is nothing but prejudice, exclusion and an arbitrary denial of one's autonomous choices in love, then the first requirement—the number restriction (two and only

FAST FACT

In 1878 the Supreme Court ruled in *Reynolds v. United States* that the constitutional guarantee of freedom of religion did not protect the right of a polygamist named George Reynolds, of Utah, to take multiple wives.

1. Meaning love among several people.

Many anti–gay rights activists believe that HBO's Big Love *(pictured), the controversial series about polygamy, will legitimize polygamy in mainstream American culture.*

two)—is a similarly arbitrary, discriminatory and indefensible denial of individual choice.

This line of argument makes gay activists furious. I can understand why they do not want to be in the same room as polygamists. But I'm not the one who put them there. Their argument does. Blogger and author Andrew Sullivan, who had the courage to advocate gay marriage at a time when it was considered pretty crazy, has called this the "polygamy diversion," arguing that homosexuality and polygamy are categorically different because polygamy is a mere "activity" while homosexuality is an intrinsic state that "occupies a deeper level of human consciousness."

Once You Start Making Distinctions . . .

But this distinction between higher and lower orders of love is precisely what gay rights activists so vigorously protest when the general culture "privileges" heterosexual unions over homosexual ones. Was *Jules et*

Jim (and [actress] Jeanne Moreau), the classic [François] Truffaut film involving two dear friends in love with the same woman, about an "activity" or about the most intrinsic of human emotions?

To simplify the logic, take out the complicating factor of gender mixing. Posit a union of, say, three gay women all deeply devoted to each other. On what grounds would gay activists dismiss their union as mere activity rather than authentic love and self-expression? On what grounds do they insist upon the traditional, arbitrary and exclusionary number of two?

Polygamy Has Stronger History than Gay Marriage

What is historically odd is that as gay marriage is gaining acceptance, the resistance to polygamy is much more powerful. Yet until this generation, gay marriage had been sanctioned by no society that we know of, anywhere at any time in history. On the other hand, polygamy was sanctioned, indeed common, in large parts of the world through large swaths of history, most notably the biblical Middle East and through much of the Islamic world.

I'm not one of those who see gay marriage or polygamy as a threat to, or assault on, traditional marriage. The assault came from within.

© 2008 Wolverton, Cagle Cartoons and PoliticalCartoons.com.

Marriage has needed no help in managing its own long, slow suicide, thank you. Astronomical rates of divorce and of single parenthood (the deliberate creation of fatherless families) existed before there was a single gay marriage or any talk of sanctioning polygamy. The minting of these new forms of marriage is a *symptom* of our culture's contemporary radical individualism—as is the decline of traditional marriage—and not its cause.

We Cannot Include Gays Without Including Polygamists

As for gay marriage, I've come to a studied ambivalence. I think it is a mistake for society to make this ultimate declaration of indifference between gay and straight life, if only for reasons of pedagogy. On the other hand, I have gay friends and feel the pain of their inability to have the same level of social approbation and confirmation of their relationship with a loved one that I'm not about to go to anyone's barricade to deny them that. It is critical, however, that any such fundamental change in the very definition of marriage be enacted democratically and not (as in the disastrous case of abortion) by judicial fiat.

Call me agnostic. But don't tell me that we can make one radical change in the one-man, one-woman rule and not be open to the claim of others that their reformation be given equal respect.

EVALUATING THE AUTHOR'S ARGUMENTS:

To make his case, Charles Krauthammer uses an argument tactic called "the slippery slope"—arguing against something by claiming it will lead to other, worse things. In your opinion, is this style of arguing effective? Why or why not?

Gay Marriage Would Not Lead to Polygamy

William Saletan

"Gays who seek to marry . . . [are] not looking for the right to sleep around. They already have that. It's called dating."

Legalizing gay marriage would not naturally lead to group marriages, argues William Saletan in the following viewpoint. In his opinion, nothing about gay marriage suggests that it would open the doors to polygamy because most human relationships are driven by jealousy, not the desire to be with multiple people. Indeed, Saletan says that most humans are too jealous to share their partner with anyone else. In fact, most polygamist relationships fail precisely because one or more of the involved parties gets jealous. Saletan also reminds Americans that gay people are not interested in getting married so they can cheat on their partner; they are seeking to get married to commit to their partner. He concludes that the polygamy argument is just a conservative tactic meant to scare Americans into disapproving of gay marriage.

Saletan is the national correspondent for the political news source Slate.com. He is also the author of *Bearing Right: How Conservatives Won the Abortion War.*

AS YOU READ, CONSIDER THE FOLLOWING QUESTIONS:
1. What does the author say was the outcome of polygamist relationships described in a *Weekly Standard* article?
2. What percent of American adults think polygamy and marital infidelity are morally acceptable, according to Saletan?
3. According to the author, what roots do jealousy, polygamy, and monogamy have in the Bible?

Uh oh. Conservatives are starting to hyperventilate again. You know the symptoms: In a haystack of right-wing dominance, they find a needle of radicalism, declare it a mortal danger to civilization, and use it to rally their voters in the next election. First it was flag-burning. Then it was the "war on Christmas." Now it's polygamy. Having crushed gay marriage nationwide in 2004, they need to gin up a new threat to the family. They've found it in *Big Love*, the HBO series about a guy with three wives. Open the door to gay marriage, they warn, and group marriage will be next.

Marriages Will Stay Between Two People Because of Jealousy

My friend Charles Krauthammer makes the argument succinctly in the *Washington Post*. "Traditional marriage is defined as the union of (1) two people of (2) opposite gender," he observes. "If, as advocates of gay marriage insist, the gender requirement is nothing but prejudice, exclusion and an arbitrary denial of one's autonomous choices," then "on what grounds do they insist upon the traditional, arbitrary and exclusionary number of two?"

Here's the answer. The number isn't two. It's one. You commit to one person, and that person commits wholly to you. Second, the number isn't arbitrary. It's based on human nature. Specifically, on jealousy.

In an excellent *Weekly Standard* article against gay marriage and polygamy, Stanley Kurtz of the Hudson Institute discusses several recent polygamous unions. In one case, "two wives agreed to allow their husbands to establish a public and steady sexual relationship." Unfortunately, "one of the wives remains uncomfortable with this arrangement," so "the story ends with at least the prospect of one marriage breaking up." In another case, "two bisexual-leaning men meet a woman and create a threesome that produces two children, one by each man." Same result: "the trio's eventual breakup."

Look up other articles on polygamy, even sympathetic ones, and you'll see the pattern. A Columbia News Service report on [the February 2006] national conference of polyamorists—people who love, but don't necessarily marry, multiple partners—features Robyn Trask, the managing editor of a magazine called *Loving More.* The conference Web site says she "has been practicing polyamory for 16 years." But according to the article, "When Trask confronted her husband about sneaking around with a long-distance girlfriend for three months, he denied it. . . . The couple is now separated and plans to divorce." A *Houston Press* article on another couple describes how "John and Brianna opened up their relationship to another woman," but "it ended badly, with the woman throwing dishes." Now they're in another threesome. "I do get jealous at times," John tells the reporter. "But not to the point where I can't flip it off."

> # FAST FACT
>
> Polygamy has not become legal or become more popular in any of the countries that have legalized same-sex marriage, such as Canada, Sweden, Denmark, South Africa, or several American states.

Jealousy Is a Natural Human Instinct

Good luck, John. I'm sure polyamorists are right that lots of people "find joy in having close relationships . . . with multiple partners." The average guy would love to bang his neighbor's wife. He just doesn't want his wife banging his neighbor. Fidelity isn't natural, but jealousy is. Hence the one-spouse rule. One isn't the number of people you want to sleep with. It's the number of people you want your spouse to sleep with.

We've been this way for a long time. Look at the Ten Commandments. One: "Thou shalt have no other gods before me." Two: "Thou shalt

The author believes gay couples such as this one want commitment and fidelity as much as straight couples do.

not make unto thee any graven image . . . Thou shalt not bow down thyself to them, nor serve them: for I the Lord thy God am a jealous God." Three: "Thou shalt not take the name of the Lord thy God in vain." In case the message isn't clear enough, the list proceeds to "Thou shalt not commit adultery" and "shalt not covet thy neighbor's wife."

Polygamy Never Ends Well

Some people say the Bible sanctions polygamy. "Abraham, David, Jacob and Solomon were all favored by God and were all polyga-mists," argues law professor Jonathan Turley. Favored? Look what polygamy did for them. Sarah told Abraham to sleep with her servant. When the servant got pregnant and came to despise Sarah, Sarah kicked her out. Rachel and Leah fought over Jacob, who ended up stripping his eldest son of his birthright for sleeping with Jacob's concubine. David got rid of Bathsheba's husband by ordering troops to betray him in battle. Promiscuity had the first word, but jealousy always had the last.

Thousands of years later, we've changed our ideas about slavery, patriarchy, and homosexuality. But we're still jealous. While 21 percent of married or divorced Americans admit to having cheated (and surveys suggest husbands are more likely than wives to stray emotionally and physically), only one in four women says she'd give a cheating husband or boyfriend a second chance, and only 5 to 6 percent of adults consider polygamy or extramarital affairs morally acceptable. As the above cases show, even people who try to practice polygamy struggle with feelings of betrayal.

Gays Want Fidelity and Commitment

Krauthammer finds the gay/poly divergence perplexing. "Polygamy was sanctioned, indeed common" for ages, he observes. "What is historically odd is that as gay marriage is gaining acceptance, the resistance to polygamy is much more powerful." But when you factor in jealousy, the oddity disappears. Women shared husbands because they had to. The alternative was poverty. As women gained power, they began to choose what they really wanted. And what they really wanted was the same fidelity that men expected from them.

Gays who seek to marry want the same thing. They're not looking for the right to sleep around. They already have that. It's called dating. A friend once explained to me why gay men have sex on the first date: Nobody says no. Your partner, being of the same sex, is as eager as you are to get it on. But he's also as eager as you are to get it on with somebody else. And if you really like him, you don't want that. You want him all to yourself. That's why marriage, not polygamy, is in your nature, and in our future.

> **EVALUATING THE AUTHOR'S ARGUMENTS:**
>
> William Saletan quotes from several sources to support the points he makes in his essay. Make a list of all the people he quotes, including their credentials and the nature of their comments. Then, analyze his use of these sources. How did Saletan factor the quotations into his argument?

Facts About Gay Marriage

Editor's note: These facts can be used in reports or papers to reinforce or add credibility when making important points or claims.

Gay Marriage in the United States

As of 2009, same-sex marriage was legal in five states:

- Massachusetts (legalized in 2003)
- Connecticut (2008)
- Iowa (2009)
- Vermont (2009)
- New Hampshire (2010)

According to the U.S. Census Bureau:

- About 100,000 official same-sex weddings, civil unions, and domestic partnerships took place in 2008.
- About 27 percent of the estimated 564,743 total gay couples report being in a marriage or a relationship akin to "husband" and "wife."
- About 91 percent of the 61.3 million total heterosexual couples reported being married.
- Of the total same-sex marriages in 2008, 56 percent were between lesbian couples.
- In 2007 about eleven thousand marriage licenses were issued to same-sex couples in the United States.

According to the Massachusetts Registry of Vital Records and Statistics, as of September 2008:

- 12,357 same-sex marriages had taken place in Massachusetts, out of 172,006 marriages in all;
- 4,539 (36 percent) of these were between male couples;
- 7,818 (64 percent) of these were between female couples;
- 6,121 weddings took place during the first year gay marriage was legalized;

- since then the rate has leveled off to about 1,500 weddings per year;
- in 2006 and 2007, this represented about 4 percent of all marriages in the state.

The U.S. Supreme Court has interfered in state laws regarding marriage just twice—to require Utah to ban the practice of polygamy in the nineteenth century, and to force sixteen states to legalize interracial marriage in 1967.

Facts About Same-Sex Couples and Their Children in the United States

According to the Williams Project on Sexual Orientation Law and Public Policy at the University of California, Los Angeles:

- Approximately 4 to 6 million Americans identify themselves as gay or lesbian.
- The five states with the highest percentage of same-sex-couple households are Vermont, California, Washington, Massachusetts, and Oregon.
- Seventy-one percent of people in same-sex couples are employed, versus 65 percent of individuals in married couples.
- In 65 percent of same-sex couples, one partner is a homeowner. By comparison, one or both partners are homeowners in 43 percent of different-sex unmarried couples and 81 percent of married couples.
- More than 39 percent of American same-sex couples are raising children.
- Same-sex American couples are raising more than 250,000 children under age eighteen.
- Same-sex parents are more likely than different-sex parents to be black and Hispanic.
- Over 46 percent of children of same-sex couples are children of color.
- Gay couples with children have fewer economic resources to care for their children than do heterosexual couples.
- Gay parents have lower household incomes, lower home-ownership rates, and lower levels of education than heterosexual parents.

- The median household income for same-sex parents in the United States is ten thousand dollars less than the median household income for heterosexual parents.
- The average household income is almost twelve thousand dollars lower.

According to the U.S. Census Bureau:

- Over 1 million American children are being raised by gay parents.
- One-quarter of the homosexual households in America contain children.

Gay Marriage Around the World

According to the British Broadcasting Corporation, as of 2009, same-sex marriage was legal in seven countries:

- Netherlands (legalized in 2001)
- Belgium (2003)
- Spain (2005)
- Canada (2005)
- South Africa (2006)
- Norway (2008)
- Sweden (2009)

Gay marriage is officially banned in nineteen countries, and such legislation has been proposed or is pending in others:

- Japan (1947)
- Cuba (1976)
- Brazil (1988)
- Bulgaria (1991)
- Paraguay (1992)
- Lithuania (1992)
- Cambodia (1993)
- Moldova (1994)
- Ukraine (1996)
- Poland (1997)
- Venezuela (1999)
- Burundi (2005)
- Honduras (2005
- Uganda (2005)
- Latvia (2005)
- Democratic Republic of Congo (2005)
- Serbia (2006)
- Ecuador (2008)
- Bolivia (2009)

American Opinions About Gay Marriage

According to a 2009 CBS News/*New York Times* poll:

- 33 percent of Americans support legal marriage for homosexual couples;
- 30 percent support civil unions for homosexual couples;
- 32 percent support no legal recognition for homosexual couples.

A 2009 poll by CNN found that 45 percent of Americans think homosexuals have a constitutional right to get married; 54 percent do not; 1 percent are unsure.

A 2009 Quinnipiac University poll found the following about American opinions of gay marriage:

- 38 percent would support a law in their state that would allow gay marriage
- 55 percent would oppose such a law

- 57 percent would support a law in their state that would allow civil unions for same-sex couples
- 38 percent would oppose such a law

- 50 percent think their state should not recognize same-sex marriages performed in other states
- 44 percent think their state should recognize same-sex marriages performed in other states

- 39 percent think gay marriage threatens traditional marriage
- 58 percent think gay marriage poses no threat to traditional marriage

- 45 percent think not allowing gay couples to marry constitutes discrimination
- 51 percent think not allowing gay couples to marry is not discriminatory

- 53 percent support allowing same-sex couples to adopt children
- 40 percent oppose allowing same-sex couples to adopt children

Most Americans do not consider same-sex marriage to be an important priority for the country. According to a 2009 NBC News/*Wall Street Journal* poll:

- Just 3 percent of Americans think same-sex marriage should be a top priority for the federal government;
- 30 percent think job creation and economic growth should be a top priority;
- 21 percent think health care should be a top priority;
- 18 percent think the deficit and government spending should be a top priority;
- 11 percent think the wars in Iraq and Afghanistan, and national security and terrorism should be top priorities;
- 4 percent said energy and the cost of gas should be a top priority.

Organizations to Contact

The editors have compiled the following list of organizations concerned with the issues debated in this book. The descriptions are derived from materials provided by the organizations. All have publications or information available for interested readers. The list was compiled on the date of publication of the present volume; the information provided here may change. Be aware that many organizations take several weeks or longer to respond to inquiries, so allow as much time as possible for the receipt of requested materials.

American Civil Liberties Union (ACLU)
132 W. Forty-third St.
New York, NY 10036
(212) 944-9800
fax: (212) 359-5290
Web site: www.aclu.org

The ACLU is the nation's oldest and largest civil liberties organization. Its Lesbian and Gay Rights/AIDS Project, started in 1986, handles litigation, education, and public policy work on behalf of gays and lesbians, and supports the legalization of same-sex marriage.

Canadian Lesbian and Gay Archives
PO Box 699, Station F
50 Charles St. East
Toronto, ON M4Y 2N6
CANADA
(416) 777-2755
Web site: http://clga.ca

This organization collects and maintains information and materials relating to the gay and lesbian rights movement in Canada and elsewhere. Its collection of records and other materials documenting the stories of lesbians and gay men and their organizations in Canada is available to the public for education and research. It also publishes the annual newsletter *Lesbian and Gay Archivist.*

Children of Lesbians and Gays Everywhere (COLAGE)
3543 Eighteenth St., Ste. 1
San Francisco, CA 94110
(415) 861-5437
fax: (415) 255-8345
e-mail: colage@colage.org
Web site: www.colage.org

COLAGE supports gay marriage on the grounds that it would be good for children. It is a national and international organization that supports young people with lesbian, gay, bisexual, and transgender (LGBT) parents. Their mission is to foster the growth of daughters and sons of LGBT parents by providing education, support, and community.

Concerned Women for America (CWFA)
1015 Fifteenth St. NW, Ste. 1100
Washington, DC 20005
(202) 488-7000
fax: (202) 488-0806
e-mail: mail@cwfa.org
Web site: www.cwfa.org

CWFA is an educational and legal defense foundation that seeks to strengthen the traditional family by promoting Judeo-Christian moral standards. It opposes gay marriage and the granting of additional civil rights protections to gays and lesbians. The CWFA publishes the monthly magazine *Family Voice* and various position papers on gay marriage and other issues.

Courage
c/o Church of St. John the Baptist
210 W. Thirty-first St.
New York, NY 10001
(212) 268-1010
fax: (212) 268-7150

e-mail: nycourage@aol.com
Web site: http://couragerc.net

Courage is a network of spiritual support groups for gay and lesbian Catholics who wish to lead celibate lives in accordance with Roman Catholic teachings on homosexuality. It publishes listings of local groups, a newsletter, and an annotated bibliography of books on homosexuality.

Family Research Council (FRC)
801 G St. NW
Washington, DC 20001
(800) 225-4008
Web site: www.frc.org

The FRC is a research, resource, and educational organization that promotes the traditional family, which it defines as a group of people bound by marriage, blood, or adoption. The council opposes gay marriage and adoption rights and publishes numerous reports from a conservative perspective on issues affecting the family, including homosexuality and same-sex marriage.

Family Research Institute (FRI)
PO Box 62640
Colorado Springs, CO 80962-0640
(303) 681-3113
Web site: www.familyresearchinst.org

The FRI distributes information about family, sexuality, and substance abuse issues. It believes that strengthening marriage would reduce many social problems, including crime, poverty, and sexually transmitted diseases. The institute publishes the bimonthly newsletter *Family Research Report* as well as numerous position papers and opinion articles.

Focus on the Family
8605 Explorer Dr.
Colorado Springs, CO 80995
(800) 232-6459
Web site: www.family.org

Focus on the Family is a conservative Christian organization that promotes traditional family values and gender roles. Its publications include the monthly magazine *Focus on the Family* and the numerous anti–gay marriage reports and articles.

Gay and Lesbian Advocates and Defenders (GLAD)
30 Winter St., Ste. 800
Boston, MA 02108
(617) 426-1350
Web site: www.glad.org

GLAD is New England's leading legal rights organization. It is dedicated to ending discrimination based on sexual orientation, HIV status, and gender identity and expression. The organization was a major supporter of same-sex marriage legalization in Connecticut, Massachusetts, New Hampshire, Maine, and Vermont.

Howard Center for Family, Religion, and Society
934 N. Main St.
Rockford, IL 61103
(815) 964-5819
Web site: http://profam.org

The purpose of the Howard Center is to provide research and understanding that demonstrates and affirms family and religion as the foundation of a virtuous and free society. The center believes that the natural family is the fundamental unit of society. The primary mission of the Howard Center is to provide a clearinghouse of useful and relevant information to support families and their defenders throughout the world. The center publishes the monthly journal *Family in America* and the *Religion and Society Report.*

Lambda Legal Defense and Education Fund, Inc.
666 Broadway, Ste. 1200
New York, NY 10012
(212) 995-8585
Web site: www.lambdalegal.org

Lambda is a public-interest law firm committed to achieving full recognition of the civil rights of homosexuals. The firm addresses a variety of areas, including equal marriage rights, the military, parenting and relationship issues, and domestic-partner benefits. It publishes the quarterly *Lambda Update* and the pamphlet *Freedom to Marry.*

National Center for Lesbian Rights

870 Market St., Ste. 570
San Francisco, CA 94102
(415) 392-6257
Web site: www.nclrights.org

The center is a public-interest law office that provides legal counseling and representation for victims of sexual-orientation discrimination. Primary areas of advice include child custody and parenting, employment, housing, the military, and insurance. The center has a section devoted to marriage rights for lesbians and gays.

National Gay and Lesbian Task Force (NGLTF)

1325 Massachusetts Ave. NW, Ste. 600
Washington, DC 20005
(202) 393-5177
Web site: www.thetaskforce.com

NGLTF is a civil rights advocacy organization that lobbies Congress and the White House on a range of civil rights issues. The organization is working to make same-sex marriage legal. It publishes numerous papers and pamphlets, the booklet *To Have and to Hold: Organizing for Our Right to Marry*, and the fact sheet "Lesbian and Gay Families."

National Organization for Marriage

20 Nassau St., Ste. 242
Princeton, NJ 08542
(609) 688-0450
e-mail: contact@nationformarriage.org
Web site: www.nationformarriage.org

This organization's mission is to protect marriage and the religious communities that sustain it. It was founded in 2007 in response to the growing movement to legalize same-sex marriage in state legislatures. It publishes numerous fact sheets, reports, and other articles on why same-sex marriage should not be legalized.

The Rockford Institute Center on the Family in America

934 N. Main St.
Rockford, IL 61103

(815) 964-5811

Web site: www.rockfordinstitute.org

The Rockford Institute works to return America to Judeo-Christian values and supports traditional roles for men and women. As such, it opposes same-sex marriage. Numerous articles on this and other issues are found in the institute's publication *Chronicles Magazine*.

Traditional Values Coalition
139 C St. SE
Washington, DC 20003
(202) 547-8570
Web site: www.traditionalvalues.org

The coalition strives to restore what the group believes are traditional moral and spiritual values in American government, schools, media, and the fiber of American society. It believes that gay rights threaten the family unit and extend civil rights beyond what the coalition considers appropriate limits. The coalition publishes the quarterly newsletter *Traditional Values Report* as well as various information papers, several of which specifically address same-sex marriage.

For Further Reading

Books

Andryszewski, Tricia. *Same-Sex Marriage: Moral Wrong or Civil Right?* Breckenridge, CO: Twenty-First Century, 2007. Puts arguments for and against same-sex marriage into a cultural, religious, political, and legal context. Good for student readers.

Badgett, M.V. Lee. *When Gay People Get Married: What Happens When Societies Legalize Same-Sex Marriage.* New York: New York University Press, 2009. Examines the potential impact of gay marriage in the United States by using data from European countries, specifically the Netherlands, where same-sex couples have had the right to marry since 2001.

Blankenhorn, David. *The Future of Marriage.* New York: Encounter, 2009. The author argues that if gay marriage is legalized, marriage as an institution will become so emptied of meaning that it will become a gender-neutral institution, rather than the premier gender-based institution of society.

Eskridge, William N., Jr., and Darren R. Spedale. *Gay Marriage: For Better or for Worse? What We've Learned from the Evidence.* New York: Oxford University Press, 2007. Uses Scandinavia's sixteen-year history of legal registered partnerships as a basis for reflection on gay marriage in the United States.

Gerstmann, Evan. *Same-Sex Marriage and the Constitution.* New York: Cambridge University Press, 2008. The author contends that one of the most important issues challenging the U.S. Constitution's promise of legal equality is same-sex marriage. Warns that legalizing these unions could be seen as an endorsement of homosexual relationships, much like legalizing heroin could be viewed as a government endorsement of drug use.

Myers, David G., and Letha Dawson Scanzoni. *What God Has Joined Together: The Christian Case for Gay Marriage.* New York: HarperOne, 2006. Presents arguments that marriage—all marriage—is good for society. Blends a traditional defense of marriage with a progressive embrace of same-sex relationships.

Polikoff, Nancy D. *Beyond (Straight and Gay) Marriage: Valuing All Families Under the Law.* Boston: Beacon, 2009. A lawyer argues that the law's narrow definitions of family and marriage no longer work in today's society.

Rauch, Jonathan. *Gay Marriage: Why It Is Good for Gays, Good for Straights, and Good for America.* New York: Times Books/Henry Holt, 2004. A leading Washington journalist argues that gay marriage is the best way to preserve and protect society's most essential institution.

Wolfson, Evan. *Why Marriage Matters: America, Equality, and Gay People's Right to Marry.* New York: Simon & Schuster, 2004. The author argues that marriage is a civil right that should be extended to gay couples.

Periodicals and Internet Sources

Abernethy, Michael. "Get Over It, Conservatives: Same-Sex Marriage Will Be Legal in All 50 States," AlterNet.org, May 19, 2009.

Antle, W. James. "Judges Not: Vermont and the New Democratic Push for Same-Sex Marriage," *American Spectator*, June 2009.

Ater, Gary. "Gay Marriage Is Approved in Maine, but Is State Approval Really on a Roll?" *American Chronicle*, May 13, 2009.

Blankenhorn, David. "Protecting Marriage to Protect Children," *Los Angeles Times*, September 19, 2008.

Breton, Marcos. "Gay Marriage Isn't Inevitable," *Sacramento (CA) Bee*, May 27, 2009.

Cohen, Phillip N. "Same-Sex Marriage and Children: What We Don't Know Shouldn't Hurt Us," Huffington Post, April 10, 2009. www.huffingtonpost.com.

Dailey, Timothy J. "Ten Facts About Counterfeit Marriage," Family Research Council. www.frc.org/content/ten-facts-about-same-sex-marriage.

Doty, Mark. "Why Do 'I Do'?" *Advocate*, October 7, 2008.

Gallagher, Maggie. "Redefinition Revolution," *National Review*, June 17, 2008.

Galli, Mark. "Is the Gay Marriage Debate Over?" *Christianity Today*, July 2009.

Haas, Jim. "Gay Marriage Is Blessing for the Economy," *San Francisco Business Times*, June 27, 2008.

Hamby, Mark. "Gavel to Gavel: Is Gay Marriage Good for Business?" *Oklahoma City Journal Record*, April 9, 2009.

Kmiec, Douglas W. and Shelley Ross Saxer. "Equality in Substance and in Name," *San Francisco Chronicle*, March 2, 2009.

Krull, Ben. "Legalizing Gay Marriage Will Make the Children Proud," *New York Daily News*, May 14, 2009.

Laituri, Logan. "The State and the Union," *Sojourners Magazine*, June 2009.

Layng, Anthony. "Where Is Marriage Going?" *USA Today* (magazine), January 2009.

Mock, Jan Vaughn. "A Letter from the Morning After," *Recorder*, November 7, 2008.

National Review, "Marriage and Civilization," May 4, 2009.

Perry, Kathryn. "The Cost of Gay Marriage," *Christian Science Monitor*, May 26, 2009.

Schlesinger, Robert. "Republican Sex Scandals a Sign It's Time to End the Family Values Wars," *U.S. News & World Report*, July 8, 2009.

Solomon, Andrew. "More Perfect Unions," *Newsweek*, January 21, 2009.

Sowell, Thomas. "Affirmative Action and Gay Marriage," *National Review*, November 4, 2008.

Spero, Aryeh. "Opposition to Gay Marriage Is Not Discrimination," *Human Events*, June 8, 2006.

Sprigg, Peter. "Homosexuality Is Not a Civil Right," Family Research Council, 2007. www.frc.org.

Steyn, Mark. "We're in the Fast Lane to Polygamy: Remember Same-Sex Marriage Proponents Rolling Their Eyes at Talk of What Might Be Next?" *MacLean's*, April 9, 2009.

Sullivan, Gregory J. "Same-Sex Marriage: Opening the Door to Polygamy," *Philadelphia Bulletin*, April 17, 2009.

Sullum, Jacob. "Gay by Force: Legal Equality Does Not Mean Requiring Universal Acceptance of Homosexuality," *Reason*, March 2009.

Suozzi, Tom. "Why I Now Support Gay Marriage," *New York Times*, June 13, 2009.

Wolf, Sherry. "The Unapologetic Case for Gay Marriage," *Socialist Worker*, November 20, 2008.

Web Sites

Against Same Sex Marriage (www.nosamesexmarriage.com). This anti–gay marriage Web site includes information on efforts to ban gay marriage in states that have legalized it.

Equal Marriage for Same-Sex Couples (www.samesexmarriage.ca). This Canadian pro–gay marriage Web site offers news updates, articles, history, legal briefs, and more.

Freedom to Marry (www.freedomtomarry.org). A gay and straight partnership working to legalize same-sex marriage. Its Web site contains maps and other useful visual information for students.

Gay Marriage News (www.gaymarriagenews.com). This site is a clearinghouse for the latest news and opinion articles about gay marriage.

Human Rights Campaign (www.hrc.org). The Web site of the nation's largest national lesbian, gay, bisexual, and transgender civil rights organization, its Marriage and Relationship Recognition section contains news, legislation, articles, and personal stories relating to gay marriage.

No Gay Marriage (www.nogaymarriage.com). This site is dedicated to preserving traditional marriage. It generates petitions that can be submitted to Congress in support of a constitutional amendment that would define marriage as between a man and a woman.

Index

rates among straight couples, 107

Domestic Partnership Act (CA, 1997), 70–71

Domestic partnerships. *See* Civil unions

E

Evan B. Donaldson Adoption Institute, 60

F

Family Research Council, 9

Fivethirtyeight.com (Web site), 28

Florida, Richard, 59

From Dawn to Decadence (Barzun), 100

G

Gallagher, Maggie, 8–9, 34

Gallup Poll, 38–39, 65, 88

Gay marriage
  countries legalizing, *46*
  as economic boom, 7, 58–59
  heterosexual marriage *vs.*, *53*
  hurts the institution of marriage, 20–21, 64–68
  hurts society, *90*
  important dates in fight over, *24*
  is inevitable, 26–33
  is not inevitable, 34–40
  nurtures children, 60–61, 105–111
  predictions on legalization of, by state, *28*
  should be legal, 12–18
  should not be legal, 19–25
  strengthens society, 92–97
  strengthens the institution of marriage, 56–63
  support for legalization of, *15, 17,* 31, 35, 38–39, 65
  threatens children, 98–104
  threatens society, 24, 85–91
  would grant rights to gay people, 69–76
  would lead to polygamy, 112–116
  would not enhance gay relationships, 48–55
  would not lead to polygamy, 117–121
  would strengthen gay relationships, 42–47
  would threaten rights of straight people, 77–83

Gershman, Jacob, 42

Goodridge, Hillary, 9

Goodridge, Julie, 9

Goodridge v. Department of Public Health (MA, 2003), 9

H

Harvey, Kenneth, 8

Heimbach, Daniel R., 19

Hilton, Perez, 38

Homophobia, 57–58

Houston Press (newspaper), 119

Hymowitz, Kay, 102

I

Incest, 51

Picture Credits

Maury Aaseng, 15, 24, 28, 46, 53, 62, 75, 81, 90, 101, 109
AP Images, 11, 44, 79, 84, 87
Art Directors & TRIP/Alamy, 50
© Bill Bachmann/Alamy, 16
Earl S. Cryer/UPI/Landov, 103
© Directphoto.org/Alamy, 66
Don Emmert/AFP/Getty Images, 41
Jonathan Ernst/Reuters/Landov, 31
© First Light/Alamy, 21
HBO/The Kobal Collection/The Picture Desk, Inc., 114
Steve Marcus/Reuters/Landov, 37
© MTP/Alamy, 120
© The Photo Works/Alamy, 61
© Queerstock, Inc./Alamy, 110
© Jim West/Alamy, 95
Kimberly White/Reuters/Landov, 72